CONTEMPORARY'S

CELEBRATE WITH US

A Beginning Reader of Holidays and Festivals

James H. Kennedy

CONTEMPORARY BOOKS

a division of NTC/CONTEMPORARY PUBLISHING COMPANY
Lincolnwood, Illinois USA

Photo Credits
Cover: American Flag, Photo Resources © Bruce Mathews; Fireworks, The Stock Solution.
Interior: Tribune File Photos, Pgs. 6, 8, 11, 13, 14, 15, 17, 19, 21, 22, 30, 36, 38, 39, 45, 46, 47, 54, 55, 61, 62, 63, 67, 70, 71, 73, 79, 87, 88, 89, 91, 96, 97, 104, 105, 111, 113, 119, 120, 121, 128, 129, 135, 136, 137, 143, 145, 152, 153, 168, 169, 170.
Picture Perfect, Pgs. 78, 112, 159.

Acknowledgments
I wish to express my appreciation to Leticia Forbes for reading and commenting on the chapters during the development of this book and to Gary Smucker for feedback on class-testing the lessons. I am indebted also to Shiniti Sakuragui for his helpful comments on the manuscript in its final stages and to Michael O'Neill and Mark Boone of Contemporary Books for their encouragement and able assistance. Finally, I am grateful to my students at the Carlos Rosario Adult Education Center in Washington, D.C., whose desire to learn about American culture inspired me to write this book. J. H. K.

Project Editor
Michael O'Neill

Library of Congress Cataloging-in-Publication Data

Kennedy, James H., 1944–
    Contemporary's celebrate with us : a beginning reader of
holidays and festivals / James H. Kennedy.
        p.   cm.
    ISBN 0-8092-3413-0
    1. Readers—Holidays. 2. English language—Textbooks for foreign
speakers. 3. Holidays—Problems, exercises, etc. 4. Festivals—
Problems, exercises, etc. I. Title.
PE1127.H85K46 1995
428.6'4—dc20   95-21466
                                                                            CIP

1997 Printing

Contents

To the Instructor

Learning about holidays and festivals celebrated in the United States is an excellent way for students of English as a Second Language to gain a better understanding of American culture. Each celebration is unique and offers students an invaluable insight into a variety of traditions and customs that have become an integral part of the cultural heritage of the United States. *Celebrate with Us* is designed to develop language skills together with cultural awareness through teaching American holiday customs, concepts, and vocabulary to adolescent and adult students at the mid-beginning level.

Each unit provides students with information about an American holiday or festival in an easy and enjoyable format. These short readings assume only limited familiarity with American customs and are designed both lexically and syntactically for beginners. While every effort has been made to keep the language natural, with the exception of special holiday terminology, vocabulary and structures are those studied in any basic first-year ESL class.

In general, *Celebrate with Us* may be used either for group study in a class or for self-study. In the classroom setting, the units offer a flexibility of use that can satisfy most teaching styles and aims. The readings and activities can be used in a variety of ways. They can be easily adapted and modified as necessary to the needs, interests, and abilities of the class.

Readings have been kept short in order to avoid overwhelming students. The aim is to reduce students' anxiety level and foster a supportive, nonthreatening atmosphere in which learners feel comfortable enough to take pleasure in reading. The format of activities and exercises is simple so that students can do them independently, in groups, or as a whole class, depending on the structure of the class and the objectives of the instructor. Exercises can be completed in class or assigned as homework.

Each unit is self-contained, so units can be used to suit individual needs and interests. An answer key for selected exercises of each unit is provided in the back of the book. The answer key not only facilitates independent study, but also gives instructors the option to do whole-class correction or to have students check their answers on their own.

Each unit contains the following sections:

- an introductory illustration and pre-reading questions
- key vocabulary
- a short reading
- comprehension exercises
- vocabulary exercises
- content review
- discussion
- writing exercises
- a think-and-discuss activity.

Illustration and Pre-Reading Questions

At the beginning of each unit, the illustration and pre-reading questions stimulate students' interest and encourage predictions about the topic of the lesson, in addition to drawing on students' own experience and prior knowledge. For most units, teachers can use the illustrations and questions in class discussion to introduce and explain key vocabulary in the reading.

Key Vocabulary

The key vocabulary precedes the reading text and presents words likely to be difficult for true mid-beginning students of English as a Second Language. Instructors can present the vocabulary in the way that best fits their teaching styles and classroom situations. Depending on students' actual knowledge, instructors may find that some words require little or no explanation; in other instances, however, additional words in the text may need explanation as well. When necessary, the primary meaning of vocabulary items should be presented as well as their significance within the holiday context. On introducing Valentine's Day, for example, teachers should present "heart" as a part of the body and as a traditional symbol of love. Since students learn vocabulary by hearing and using words frequently, key vocabulary items in the readings reappear several times in the exercises. This reinforcement promotes vocabulary retention.

Reading

The reading can first be read silently by students or read by the instructor as students follow along. Students should underline unfamiliar vocabulary. During the reading, the instructor may wish to pause periodically to ask brief questions about vocabulary and content. If time permits, students can read the text aloud for additional practice and vocabulary reinforcement.

Comprehension Exercises

The first part of these exercises is a true-false section that checks comprehension without forcing students to write. Students with limited writing skills should have no trouble here. The second part of the comprehension exercises verifies comprehension through a minimum of writing: students write a single word to correct each sentence. Students should do both of these exercises without referring to the reading passage.

New Words and More Word Work

There are two vocabulary activities: **New Words** and **More Word Work.** The New Words exercise is designed to help students retain newly learned vocabulary through reinforcement. To lower the inhibitions of students with weak writing skills, writing here is kept to a minimum also: from a list of vocabulary, students select a word that completes each sentence. The key words in this exercise are always treated as they relate specifically to the context of the unit.

More Word Work

This section includes two activities for additional opportunity to work with useful and important words from the reading. Again, the emphasis is on reinforcement of vocabulary and comprehension. Varying from unit to unit, the exercises include activities such as crossword puzzles, word association, and word-search exercises. In a number of units, exercises require students to work not only with words in the reading, but with related vocabulary as well.

Content Review

The content review is a cloze exercise that students should be encouraged to do without looking at the reading. The words used to fill in the blanks need not be the same as those in the story; the important thing is for the sentences to be correct.

Discussion

This section comprises questions for students to answer orally, though instructors may also wish to use them as the basis for writing exercises by having students write out the answers either during class time or for homework. The questions not only check comprehension and reinforce vocabulary, but also give students the opportunity to share information about their own experiences, celebrations, and customs with their classmates. For this reason, questions include items that elicit personal comments in order to foster classroom discussion, stimulate cross-cultural exchange, and enhance self-esteem as well as multicultural awareness.

Writing

Writing activities give students structured practice in writing words and short sentences. Simple in format, these exercises are appropriate for students with low-level or no writing skills, as well as for those who have little experience with the Roman alphabet. Beginners should be able to complete these activities without great difficulty.

Think and Discuss

These activities are open-ended questions for which, in most cases, there are no right or wrong answers. The questions stimulate students' curiosity and encourage them to discuss concepts related to the lesson context. The activities foster the development and use of critical thinking skills in English; students draw not only on their linguistic knowledge but on their contextual knowledge as well.

In classroom testing of *Celebrate with Us*, average beginning ESL students have found this text easy to use and essential to their success in developing the confidence necessary for acquiring strong language skills. *Celebrate with Us* has been used effectively with students of limited education and literacy as well as with more educated and literate beginners. It is the author's hope that through the study of these cultural units, students will gain an understanding of the concepts and traditions associated with our most widely celebrated holidays and festivals. With the cultural insights provided in these units, students should broaden their knowledge and understanding of American society and, consequently, be able to participate more effectively in it and enjoy life in the United States more fully.

HOLIDAYS

Look at these pictures. Why do you think these people are happy?

Look at a calendar. Is there a holiday this month?

Do you like holidays? Why or why not?

Learn these words with your teacher.

event	festival	enjoy
celebration	immigrants	religious
picnic	celebrate	

Holidays

Holidays are special days. Most holidays are days to remember important people and events. In the United States, there is a holiday in almost every month of the year.

Banks, offices, and schools do not open on some holidays. These days are national holidays. Most people do not work and students do not go to school on national holidays. Three national holidays in the United States are Independence Day, Presidents' Day, and Labor Day.

Some holidays are special religious days. Christmas and Easter are important religious holidays. Some holidays are festivals from other countries. Immigrants brought the celebration of Chinese New Year and Mardi Gras to the United States many years ago. Now many Americans enjoy these holidays every year.

A holiday is usually a time for a happy celebration. People have parties or picnics with friends on some holidays. On other holidays people stay at home and celebrate with their families.

Everybody likes a holiday. Don't you?

1 Comprehension

A. Circle <u>yes</u> or <u>no</u> after each sentence.

1.	People have picnics on some holidays.	(Yes)	No
2.	Independence Day is a national holiday.	Yes	No
3.	Most people work on Labor Day.	Yes	No
4.	Schools do not open on some holidays.	Yes	No
5.	Presidents' Day is a religious holiday.	Yes	No
6.	Banks and offices open on national holidays.	Yes	No
7.	Immigrants brought Labor Day to the United States.	Yes	No

Now show your answers to another student. Are your answers the same or different? Why?

B. One word in each sentence is wrong. Find the word and cross it out. Then write the correct word.

1. Most holidays are days to remember important ~~schools~~ *people* and events.
2. Banks, picnics, and schools do not open on some holidays.
3. In the United States, there is a holiday in almost every week of the year.
4. Independence Day and Labor Day are religious holidays.
5. Friends brought the celebration of Mardi Gras to the United States many years ago.
6. A holiday is usually a time for a sad celebration.

2 New Words

Choose one of the following words to complete each sentence. You can work with a classmate.

celebrate   religious   celebrations
immigrants   events   picnic

1. Christmas is an important _religious_ holiday.

2. We remember important _____ on some holidays.

3. Holidays are times for special _____.

4. Most people _____ Christmas with their families.

5. _____ brought Mardi Gras to the United States many years ago.

6. Some people like to have a _____ with their friends on a holiday.

3 More Word Work

A. Find the words. Some words go across. Some words go down.

```
R E L I C E L B R A N J O      Celebrate
P I C N D C A R P M B T S      Easter
F Y D M V E A S T E R Z L      Enjoy
E P E O P L E P A R T Y U      Event
S O M I R E L I G I O U S      Festival
T F E S T B A C E L E B R      Immigrants
I M M I G R A N T S N I V      National
V P E O P A N I P I J N I      Party
A E V E N T H C I M O I G      People
L I G I C E L E B R Y G T      Picnic
N J O Y E V E P I C N I Y      Religious
P N A T I O N A L M R E L
```

B. Cross out the word that does not belong.

1. Christmas   Easter   ~~American~~   Labor Day
2. event   year   day   month
3. festival   holiday   picnic   celebration
4. students   parties   friends   immigrants
5. bank   school   office   work

4 Content Review

With a classmate, complete the sentences. Fill each blank with one word.

Everybody likes holidays. Most holidays are _special_ days to remember important _____ and events. On national holidays _____, offices, and schools do not _____. Labor Day is a national _____. Christmas and Easter are important _____ holidays. A holiday is a time for _____.

5 Discussion

What are the answers to these questions? Discuss your answers with another student.

1. How do people celebrate holidays?
2. What day is a national holiday in the United States?
3. Do schools open on national holidays?
4. What day is a religious holiday in the United States?
5. Do you like holidays? Why?
6. What day is a national holiday in your country?
7. What day is a religious holiday in your country?
8. Do you like picnics?
9. When do you like to have picnics?
10. When do people in your country have parties?

6 Writing

1. Write the name of your country.

   Example: *My country is Brazil.*

   _____

2. Write the name of a national holiday in your country.

   Example: *Independence Day is a national holiday in Brazil.*

   _____

3. Write the name of a religious holiday in your country.

   Example: *Christmas is a religious holiday in Brazil.*

   _____

4. Write the name of a holiday that you like very much in your country.

Example: *I like Carnival very much.*

_____

7 Think and Discuss

Think about these questions. Then discuss your answers with the class.

1. What is your favorite holiday?
2. What are the special things that you do on this holiday?
3. Why do you like this holiday?

BEW ILLINOIS AFL CIO L

LABOR DAY

Find the month of September on a calendar.
What is the date of Labor Day?

Are the people in the pictures working?

What are they doing?

Are they happy or sad?

Learn these words with your teacher.

labor	barbecue	honor
rest	vacation	return
fun	parade	labor union
sale		

Labor Day

The first Monday in September is Labor Day in the United States. Labor means work. Labor Day is the holiday that honors workers. On this day, Americans remember that all workers are very important. Carpenters, secretaries, mechanics, engineers, and many other people do not work on Labor Day. Schools, banks, and offices do not open.

Labor Day is a day of rest and fun for most people. In many cities and towns, labor unions celebrate this holiday with parades. Many stores have special sales. The weather is usually warm, and people have fun at picnics and barbecues.

Labor Day is one of the last days of the summer vacation season. Soon the weather will be cold. Soon most public parks, swimming pools, and beaches will close until the month of May. Students usually return to school the day after Labor Day.

1 Comprehension

A. Circle yes or no after each sentence.

1. Labor Day is the first Monday in September.	(Yes)	No
2. Many people do not work on Labor Day.	Yes	No
3. Banks open on Labor Day.	Yes	No
4. Americans honor workers on Labor Day.	Yes	No
5. People celebrate Labor Day with picnics.	Yes	No
6. It is usually cold on Labor Day.	Yes	No
7. Labor unions have sales on Labor Day.	Yes	No
8. Workers are important.	Yes	No

Now show your answers to another student. Are your answers the same or different? Why?

B. One word in each sentence is wrong. Find the word and cross it out. Then write the correct word.

1. The first ~~Wednesday~~ *Monday* in September is Labor Day in the United States.
2. Labor Day is the holiday that honors schools.
3. Secretaries and mechanics do not remember on Labor Day.
4. Schools, stores, and banks do not open.
5. People have fun at work and barbecues.
6. Many stores have special parades.

2 New Words

Choose one of the words or the group of words below to complete each sentence. You can work with a classmate.

sales	return	labor unions
honors	fun	rest

1. Labor Day is a day of ____*rest*____ for many workers.
2. People have _____ at barbecues.
3. Labor Day _____ workers.
4. Students _____ to school after Labor Day every year.
5. Many stores have special _____ on Labor Day.
6. _____ have parades in many cities on Labor Day.

3 More Word Work

A. Find these words in the story about "Labor Day." Draw a line under them. Then look for the opposites of these words in the story. Circle the opposites. Write the opposites here.

1. work   ___*rest*___   3. open   _____

2. warm   _____   4. first   _____

B. Cross out the word that does not belong.

1. beach	~~engineer~~	park	swimming pool
2. weather	parade	picnic	barbecue
3. rest	fun	vacation	work
4. worker	carpenter	labor	mechanic
5. many	last	most	all
6. school	office	secretary	store

4 Content Review

With a classmate, complete the sentences. Fill each blank with one word.

Labor Day is the first ___*Monday*___ in September. It is the

_____ that honors workers every year. Many

_____ do not work on Labor _____ .

Schools and banks do not _____ . Many people

have fun at _____ and barbecues. Students often return to

_____ the day after Labor Day.

5 Discussion

What are the answers to these questions? Discuss your answers with another student.

1. In what season do students usually have vacation?
2. In what month do students return to school in the United States?
3. When do students return to school in your country?
4. Why do people buy things on Labor Day?
5. What is the date of Labor Day this year?
6. Does your country celebrate Labor Day? When?
7. Are you a worker? What is your occupation?
8. Where do you work?
9. Do you think your work is important? Why?

6 Writing

A. Write the occupations of four people who work in your school.

Example: *teacher*

1. _____   3. _____

2. _____   4. _____

Write the occupations of six of your classmates.

1. _____   4. _____

2. _____   5. _____

3. _____   6. _____

Write the occupations of people in your family.

1. _____   3. _____

2. _____   4. _____

B. Write the answers to these questions.

1. What is your occupation?

    Example: *I am a secretary.*

    _____

2. Where do you work?

    _____

3. When do you have vacation?

_____

4. Why do you work?

_____

7 Think and Discuss

Think about these questions. Then discuss your ideas with the class.

A. What is a good worker? Why do people like good workers?

B. Can you explain this popular expression?
"All work and no play makes Jack a dull boy."

COLUMBUS DAY

Look at the month of October on a calendar. What is the date of Columbus Day?

Look at a map. Can you find Spain and India?

Is Spain near or far from India?

What are the people in the pictures doing?

Learn these words with your teacher.

explorer	spice	trip
island	sailor	travel
jewel	sea	dangerous

Columbus Day

Columbus Day is the second Monday in October. The traditional date is October 12. This day honors Christopher Columbus's first trip to America in 1492.

Columbus was born in Italy. Before his famous trip, he was a sailor. He also made maps. In those days, Europeans liked to buy spices, jewels, and other things from China and India. People had to travel by land to go to these countries. These trips were long and dangerous. Columbus wanted to find a short way to China and India by sea. The king and queen of Spain gave him money for his trip. Columbus left Spain with three ships. Two months later, on October 12, 1492, he arrived at an island near North America.

Columbus did not know that there was land between Europe and Asia. He was in America, but he thought that he was in India. For that reason, he called the people on the island Indians. After Columbus's trip many explorers traveled from Europe to see America. Many people from France, Spain, England, and other countries came to live in America.

Columbus Day is a holiday in most states. A few days before the holiday, students usually read and learn about Columbus. Then, on Columbus Day, schools do not open. Cities have parades and other special events to honor Christopher Columbus.

1 Comprehension

A. Circle yes or no after each sentence.

1. Columbus Day is a holiday in October.	(Yes)	No
2. Columbus was born in Spain.	Yes	No
3. Columbus first traveled to America in 1492.	Yes	No
4. People in Europe liked to buy spices from India.	Yes	No
5. Trips to China were short.	Yes	No
6. Columbus was a sailor before his trip to America.	Yes	No
7. Columbus arrived at an island in India in 1492.	Yes	No
8. After Columbus's trip, many Europeans traveled to America.	Yes	No

Now show your answers to another student. Are your answers the same or different? Why?

B. One word in each sentence is wrong. Find the word and cross it out. Then write the correct word.

1. Columbus was a sailor before his trip to ~~India~~. *America*
2. Europeans liked to buy ships and other things from China and India.
3. Columbus wanted to find a long way to China and India by sea.
4. The king and queen of Italy gave Columbus money for his trip.
5. Columbus did not know that there was land between America and Asia.
6. Columbus left Spain with two ships.
7. He arrived at an island near North America on August 12, 1492.
8. After Columbus's trip, many Indians came from Europe to live in America.

2 New Words

Choose one of the following words to complete each sentence. You can work with a classmate.

dangerous   island   spices

explorers   sailor   travel

1. After Columbus's trip to America, many __explorers__ came from Europe to see America.

2. Christopher Columbus arrived at an _____ on October 12, 1492.

3. Europeans had to _____ by land to China.

4. In the days of Columbus, trips to India were very _____.

5. Before Columbus traveled to America, he was a _____.

6. People in Europe liked _____ from India.

3 More Word Work

A. Find the words. Some words go across. Some words go down.

```
S I M K L U D S H I P I
A N A M E R I C A Y C T
I D P L X M S O I F O A
L I M U P K V L N R L L
O A S A L C A U D A E Y
R N E M O H N M I N X S
U S A P R I P B A S P A
D A N G E R O U S A I L
W I T A R Y V S P I C E
L O C H F N A D Y N O L
K I N G I S L A N D H Y
A B U S P A I N E X D E
```

America

Columbus

Dangerous

Explorer

India

Indians

Island

Italy

King

Sailor

Sea

Ship

Spice

B. Cross out the word that does not belong.

1. England   Spain   ~~Asia~~   India
2. queen   island   student   explorer
3. country   city   state   spice
4. sea   king   ship   sailor
5. trip   between   after   before
6. date   land   day   month

4 Content Review

With a classmate, complete the sentences. Fill each blank with one word.

Columbus Day honors Christopher Columbus's first ___*trip*___ to America. Columbus was born in _____. Before his trip, he was a _____. Columbus wanted to find a short _____ to India by sea. He left _____ with three ships. He arrived at an _____ on October 12, 1492. Columbus called the people there _____ because he thought that he was in _____. After Columbus's trip, many Europeans came to _____ in America.

5 Discussion

What are the answers to these questions? Discuss your answers with another student.

1. When is Columbus Day?
2. Who was Columbus?
3. Where was he born?
4. Who were the Indians that Columbus saw in America?
5. What is the date of the Columbus Day celebration this year?
6. Why is Columbus Day in October?
7. Is October 12 a holiday in your country? What is the name of the holiday?

6 Writing

A. People in the United States buy many things from other countries. Write the names of five things that you like from other countries. Write the names of the countries also.

Example: *cars*   *Japan*

1. _____   _____
2. _____   _____
3. _____   _____
4. _____   _____
5. _____   _____

B. Columbus was born in Italy. He was Italian. The queen of Spain gave Columbus money. The queen was Spanish. Write the nationalities for the following countries.

Country	Nationality
1. Italy	*Italian*
2. Spain	_____
3. England	_____
4. France	_____
5. India	_____
6. China	_____
7. Mexico	_____
8. Vietnam	_____
9. Brazil	_____
10. Korea	_____

C. Write the questions to these answers.

1. When ___is Columbus Day___?

    Columbus Day is the second Monday in October.

2. Where _____?

    He was born in Italy.

3. What _____?

    They liked to buy spices and other things from India.

4. What _____?

    They gave him money for his trip.

5. When _____?

    Columbus arrived there on October 12, 1492.

7 Think and Discuss

Think about these questions. Then discuss your ideas with the class.

A. Over 100 years ago, a Native American leader named Tecumseh said, "These lands are ours. No one has the right to remove us because we were the first owners." Can you explain this statement? Discuss your ideas with the class.

B. Some Americans do not celebrate Columbus Day. Do you know why? Discuss your ideas with the class.

HALLOWEEN

Find the month of October on a calendar. What is the date of Halloween?

Are the people in these pictures young or old?

What are they wearing?

Do you think they are happy or sad?

Learn these words with your teacher.

mask	witch	jack-o'-lantern
costume	ghost	decoration
pumpkin	adult	symbol
candle		

Halloween

Every year, Americans celebrate Halloween on October 31. On this day, young people wear masks and costumes. Boys and girls dress as witches, ghosts, and other characters. Children like to wear their costumes to school, where there is often a special party.

In the evening, children wear their costumes and carry bags to their neighbors' houses. The children knock, and when the neighbor opens the door, they shout, "Trick or treat!" Then the neighbor puts fruit or candy in the children's bags.

Halloween decorations are usually orange and black, the traditional colors for this special day. A popular symbol of Halloween is the jack-o'-lantern. To make a jack-o'-lantern, children's parents usually cut a face in a pumpkin and put a candle inside.

In large cities, adults enjoy Halloween also. Many adults wear masks and costumes and have parties at night.

1 Comprehension

A. Circle <u>yes</u> or <u>no</u> after each sentence.

1. The jack-o'-lantern is a symbol of Halloween. **Yes** **No**
2. Halloween is the last day of October. **Yes** **No**
3. The colors for Halloween are red and black. **Yes** **No**
4. Children give candy to their neighbors in the evening. **Yes** **No**
5. Adults have Halloween parties in large cities. **Yes** **No**
6. Children wear masks on Halloween. **Yes** **No**

Now show your answers to another student. Are your answers the same or different? Why?

B. One word in each sentence is wrong. Find the word and cross it out. Then write the correct word.

1. Americans celebrate Halloween every year on ~~August~~ *October* 31.
2. On this day, young people eat masks and costumes.
3. Boys and girls dress as witches, candles, and other characters.
4. Children like to wear their symbols to school.
5. Halloween decorations are usually orange and blue.
6. Children wear their costumes and carry fruit to their neighbors' houses.
7. The costume is a popular symbol of Halloween.
8. Children's parents cut a face in a bag and put a candle inside.

2 New Words

Choose one of the following words to complete each sentence. You can work with a classmate.

pumpkin   costumes   decorations
symbol   candle   adults

1. In large cities, many adults wear ____*costumes*____ at night.
2. The orange and black _____ are for our Halloween party.
3. There is usually a _____ inside a jack-o'-lantern.
4. We cut a face in a _____ to make a jack-o'-lantern.
5. _____ in large cities have parties on Halloween night.
6. The jack-o'-lantern is a _____ of Halloween.

3 More Word Work

A. Cross out the word that does not belong.

1. girls   boys   ~~adults~~   children
2. candy   face   pumpkin   fruit
3. night   bag   evening   day
4. orange   black   pumpkin   jack-o'-lantern
5. parents   people   symbol   neighbors

B. Complete the puzzle.

Across

3. The last day of _____ is Halloween.

9. Halloween _____ are usually orange and black.

11. On Halloween evening, children carry _____ to their neighbors' houses.

14. We cut a face in a _____ to make a popular symbol of Halloween.

15. October 31 is _____.

Down

1. Neighbors put candy and _____ in the children's bags.

2. Parents cut a _____ in a pumpkin to make a jack-o'-lantern.

4. There is usually a _____ inside a jack-o'-lantern.

5. Halloween is the special day that children wear costumes and _____.

6. Children _____ bags to their neighbors' houses on Halloween night.

7. On Halloween, there is usually a _____ for young children at school.

8. Neighbors give candy to girls and _____ on Halloween.

10. The young student wants to wear her Halloween _____ to school.

12. Adults in big cities sometimes _____ costumes on Halloween.

13. Boys and girls knock on their neighbor's _____ at night.

4 Content Review

With a classmate, complete the sentences. Fill each blank with one word.

Americans celebrate Halloween on October 31 __*every*__ year. Boys and girls wear masks and _____ on this special day. At night, children _____ on their neighbors' doors and shout, "_____ or treat!" Then the neighbors put _____ or fruit in the children's bags.

The _____ is a popular symbol of Halloween.

_____ and black are the traditional colors for Halloween.

5 Discussion

What are the answers to these questions? Discuss your answers with another student.

1. When is Halloween?
2. What do children wear on Halloween?
3. What do they do in the evening?
4. Why do children carry bags in the evening?
5. What are the traditional colors for Halloween?
6. Does your country have a day like Halloween? When?
7. When do children wear costumes in your country?
8. When do adults wear costumes in your country?
9. When do people in your country give fruit or candy to children?

6 Writing

Write the names of five fruits that you like. Then write the colors of these fruits.

	Fruit	Color
Example:	*banana*	*yellow*
1.	_____	_____
2.	_____	_____
3.	_____	_____
4.	_____	_____
5.	_____	_____

Now write the names and colors of three fruits that you do not like.

1. _____   _____
2. _____   _____
3. _____   _____

Write three things that children do on Halloween.

1. _____
2. _____
3. _____

7 Think and Discuss

Think about these questions. Then discuss your ideas with the class.

A. You are going to a Halloween party. Everyone has to wear a costume to the party. What costume will you wear? Why?

B. Why do you think people like to wear costumes on Halloween?

VETERANS DAY

Look at a calendar. What is the date of Veterans Day?

What do you see in the pictures?

What are these people doing?

What are they wearing?

Learn these words with your teacher.

Army	peace	march
Air Force	war	patriotic
Marines	soldier	uniform
Navy		

Veterans Day

November 11 is Veterans Day. Veterans are people who fought in wars. Americans first celebrated Veterans Day to remember the end of World War I on November 11, 1918. They wanted to honor the soldiers who fought in that war. They wanted also to celebrate peace. After World War I, the United States fought in other wars. So now Americans remember all veterans on this day.

Veterans Day is a national holiday. It is usually on a Monday in some states. On this holiday, Americans honor veterans of the United States Army, Navy, Air Force, and Marines. The special colors of the day are red, white, and blue—the colors of the American flag.

Americans celebrate Veterans Day in various ways. Many veterans wear their old uniforms and march in parades. Many people go to watch the parades. Some people go to cemeteries on this day. Many people go shopping because stores have big sales on Veterans Day. But some people do not go out at all. They stay home and rest. Many people put American flags in front of their homes to celebrate this important, patriotic holiday.

1 Comprehension

A. Circle yes or no after each sentence.

1.	November 11 is a national holiday.	(Yes)	No
2.	Americans remember veterans on November 11.	Yes	No
3.	Veterans are people who march in wars.	Yes	No
4.	Veterans Day is a patriotic holiday.	Yes	No
5.	There are parades on Veterans Day.	Yes	No
6.	Stores do not open on Veterans Day.	Yes	No

Now show your answers to another student. Are your answers the same or different? Why?

B. One word in each sentence is wrong. Find the word and cross it out. Then write the correct word.

1. Veterans Day is ~~December~~ *November* 11.
2. Veterans are people who fought in stores.
3. Many people put American uniforms in front of their homes to celebrate Veterans Day.
4. Veterans Day is a religious holiday.
5. The special colors of this holiday are red, white, and black.
6. Many veterans march in cemeteries on Veterans Day.
7. Stores have big uniforms on Veterans Day.
8. Some people stay home and work on Veterans Day.

2 New Words

Choose one of the following words to complete each sentence. You can work with a classmate.

parades	war	peace	uniforms
veterans	soldiers	patriotic	

1. ___*Soldiers*___ who fought in wars are veterans.
2. Americans honor _____ on November 11.
3. At the end of World War I, people celebrated _____.
4. Veterans Day is a _____ holiday.
5. Many people like to watch _____ on this day.
6. Many veterans like to wear their old _____ on Veterans Day.
7. There was a big celebration at the end of the _____.

3 More Word Work

A. Find the words. Some words go across. Some words go down.

```
N A V U N I F A R M V E T        Army
F P L N A V Y R E S F U P        Cemetery
L E C E M E T E R Y L I A        Flag
M A P A R T N S V H A N T        Honor
A H A R M E K T E O W I R        March
R O R M A R C H T N A F I        Marines
I N A P E A C E E O R M O        Navy
N R D E U N I F O R M A T        Parade
E M E A M S F L A G Y M I        Patriotic
S Y R E S V E T E R A R C        Peace
F L A W A R P A T R I O R        Uniform
P A R A D M A R C K V E Y        Veterans
                                 War
```

B. Cross out the word that does not belong.

1. white	blue	~~peace~~	red
2. out	many	various	all
3. Army	Marines	Navy	November
4. veterans	Americans	sales	soldiers
5. celebrate	honor	remember	wear
6. shopping	stay	store	sale

4 Content Review

With a classmate, complete the sentences. Fill each blank with one word.

Veterans Day is a national ___*holiday*___. Veterans are people who fought in _____. The special colors for Veterans Day are _____, white, and blue. Americans honor veterans and _____ peace on this day. Many veterans _____ in parades. Many people put American _____ in front of their homes. Veterans _____ is an important, patriotic holiday.

5 Discussion

What are the answers to these questions? Discuss your answers with another student.

1. What is a veteran?
2. Who do we honor on Veterans Day?
3. How do Americans celebrate this holiday?
4. Why do some people go to cemeteries on Veterans Day?
5. Does your country have a special day to honor soldiers or veterans? When is it?
6. What happens on that day?
7. Does your country have a special day to celebrate peace? When?
8. When do people in your country put flags in front of their homes?
9. Are you a veteran? Are there veterans in your family?
10. What Veterans Day activities are there in this city?
11. Is there a war now? Where?

6 Writing

A. Ask five classmates about the flags of their countries. Write the information below.

	Country	Color of Flag
Example:	U.S.A.	red, white, blue
1.	_____	_____
2.	_____	_____
3.	_____	_____
4.	_____	_____
5.	_____	_____

B. Put the words in the correct order.

1. _Veterans Day is in November._ _____

   in   Day   is   November   Veterans

2. _____

   holiday   patriotic   Day   a   is   Veterans

3. _____

   march   in   many   parades   veterans

4. _____

   front   their   people   put   of   homes   flags   in

5. _____

   fought   people   wars   in   who   are   veterans

7 Think and Discuss

Think about these questions. Then discuss your ideas with the class.

A. Why does a country need a good army and navy?

B. Benjamin Franklin, one of the first diplomats of the United States, once said, "There was never a good war or a bad peace." What do you think this means? Do you agree?

THANKSGIVING DAY

Find November on a calendar. What is the date of Thanksgiving Day this year?

What do you see in the pictures?

What are these people doing?

Learn these words with your teacher.

Native Americans	die	invite
Pilgrims	hunt	show
turkey		

Thanksgiving Day

Americans celebrate Thanksgiving Day on the fourth Thursday in November. On this holiday, people give thanks for all the good things in their lives.

The Pilgrims celebrated the first Thanksgiving Day in Massachusetts over 300 years ago. The Pilgrims were immigrants from England. Their trip to America was long and difficult. They traveled on a ship for more than two months. When they arrived in Massachusetts in December 1620, many people were sick.

The Pilgrims' first year in America was very difficult. The winter was terrible. They had to build their houses. They did not have much food. They were cold and hungry. Many people died. In the spring, Native Americans helped the Pilgrims. They showed the Pilgrims how to plant corn, catch fish, and hunt. After one year in America, the Pilgrims celebrated with a big dinner. They invited their friends, the Native Americans, to eat and celebrate with them.

Today Thanksgiving is a family holiday. People who live far away visit their families for the celebration. Many people go to church in the morning. Then, in the afternoon, they eat the traditional Thanksgiving dinner: turkey, cranberry sauce, sweet potatoes, corn, and pumpkin pie.

1 Comprehension

A. Circle yes or no after each sentence.

1. Thanksgiving Day is in November. — Yes   No
2. Americans celebrate Thanksgiving Day with a special dinner. — Yes   No
3. The Native Americans invited the Pilgrims to the first Thanksgiving celebration. — Yes   No
4. Americans celebrate Thanksgiving with their families. — Yes   No
5. The Native Americans were immigrants from England. — Yes   No

Now show your answers to another student. Are your answers the same or different? Why?

B. One word in each sentence is wrong. Find the word and cross it out. Then write the correct word.

1. Americans celebrate Thanksgiving on the ~~first~~ *fourth* Thursday in November.
2. The Pilgrims celebrated the first Thanksgiving over 300 months ago.
3. The Pilgrims were immigrants from America.
4. They were cold and hungry in the spring.
5. Native immigrants showed the Pilgrims how to plant corn.
6. The Pilgrims invited the Native Americans to eat and hunt with them.
7. Today people who live far away visit their friends for the celebration of Thanksgiving.

2 New Words

Choose one of the following words or group of words to complete each sentence. You can work with a classmate.

showed	turkey	immigrants
died	Native Americans	

1. The Native Americans _*showed*_ the Pilgrims how to catch fish.
2. The Pilgrims were _____ from England.
3. Many Pilgrims were sick and _____ in the winter.
4. On Thanksgiving Day, Americans usually eat _____.
5. The _____ showed the Pilgrims how to plant corn.

3 More Word Work

A. Cross out the word that does not belong.

1. England   America   ~~Pilgrim~~   Massachusetts
2. dinner   corn   pumpkin   cranberry
3. cold   sick   hunt   hungry
4. Pilgrim   immigrant   Thanksgiving   American

B. Complete this puzzle.

Across

3. The Pilgrims lived in _____ over 300 years ago.
6. Americans usually have _____ for dinner on Thanksgiving Day.
7. The Pilgrims celebrated the first Thanksgiving over 300 _____ ago.
9. On this holiday, people give thanks for all the _____ things in their lives.
12. The Pilgrims were _____ from England.

Down

1. Native Americans showed the Pilgrims how to _____.
2. _____ is a popular American holiday in November.

4. Americans often eat turkey with cranberry _____ .
5. Thanksgiving Day is always on a _____ .
8. Thanksgiving day is the fourth Thursday in _____ .
10. Native Americans showed the Pilgrims how to plant _____ .
11. Native Americans showed the Pilgrims how to catch _____ .

C. Look at these words.

Massachusetts	turkey	pumpkin pie	America
cranberry sauce	fish	winter	family
sweet potato	church	England	corn

Which words are places? Which words are kinds of food? Make two lists. You cannot use every word.

Places	Food
England	*turkey*
_____	_____
_____	_____
_____	_____
_____	_____

4 Content Review

Americans give thanks for the good things in their lives on *Thanksgiving* Day. This popular holiday is always the _____ Thursday in November. The Pilgrims celebrated the _____ Thanksgiving Day with Native Americans over 300 years _____ . Most Americans today celebrate this holiday with their _____ . The traditional foods for Thanksgiving dinner are: _____ , cranberry sauce, sweet potatoes, corn, and _____ pie.

5 Discussion

What are the answers to these questions? Discuss your answers with another student.

1. When is Thanksgiving Day?
2. What is the date of Thanksgiving Day this year?
3. Who celebrated the first Thanksgiving Day?
4. Who were the Pilgrims?
5. When did the Pilgrims celebrate the first Thanksgiving Day?
6. What do Americans eat on Thanksgiving Day?
7. Do you have a day like Thanksgiving Day in your country?
8. Do you celebrate Thanksgiving Day in the United States? How do you celebrate it?

6 Writing

A. Thanksgiving Day is a time to give thanks for the good things in our lives. Make a list of five good things in your life.

1. _____
2. _____
3. _____
4. _____
5. _____

B. Write the questions to these answers.

1. When *did the Pilgrims come from England* ?
   The Pilgrims came from England in 1620.

2. When _____?
   Americans celebrate Thanksgiving Day on the fourth Thursday in November.

3. Where _____?

The Pilgrims celebrated the first Thanksgiving Day in Massachusetts.

4. Who _____?

The Native Americans showed the Pilgrims how to hunt.

7 Think and Discuss

Think about these questions. Then discuss your ideas with the class.

A. Imagine that three classmates are going to have Thanksgiving dinner at your home. You want to serve American food and also something typical of your country. What foods will you serve?

B. A famous American president named Franklin Delano Roosevelt once said, "All of our people all over the country—except the Indians—are immigrants or descendants of immigrants." Can you explain this famous statement? Discuss your ideas with the class.

Cranberry Sauce

4 cups cranberries
1 cup water
1 cup sugar

Put cranberries, water, and sugar into a saucepan. Boil slowly for 10 minutes. Remove from fire and cool. Put cranberry sauce in refrigerator until ready to serve.

HANUKKAH

What do you see in these pictures?

What are the people doing?

Are they happy or sad?

Learn these words and expressions with your teacher.

applesauce	Jewish	get together
hymn	pancake	no wonder

Hanukkah

Hanukkah is a very happy festival that Jewish families celebrate every winter. Jewish people celebrate Hanukkah for eight nights, usually in the month of December. For Jewish children of all ages, Hanukkah is one of the happiest times of the year. They enjoy this festival very much.

Another name for Hanukkah is the Festival of Lights. To celebrate Hanukkah, Jewish families get together and light candles on eight nights. They light one candle the first night and two candles on the second night. On the third night, they light three candles. They light one more candle each night until the eighth night, when they light eight candles.

After each evening's candle lighting ceremony, families sing a hymn and traditional songs. Then everybody eats special foods, especially potato pancakes, applesauce, and cheese. Children have fun playing traditional games. Also, on each night of Hanukkah, parents give money, candy, books, and other small gifts to their children. No wonder children enjoy Hanukkah!

1 Comprehension

A. Circle yes or no after each sentence.

1. Hanukkah is usually in December.	**Yes**	**No**
2. Jewish children enjoy Hanukkah very much.	**Yes**	**No**
3. On the fourth night of Hanukkah, Jewish families light two candles.	**Yes**	**No**
4. Hanukkah is a sad festival.	**Yes**	**No**
5. The Festival of Lights is another name for Hanukkah.	**Yes**	**No**
6. After the candle lighting ceremony, children give their parents money and other gifts.	**Yes**	**No**

7. Jewish people light six candles on the
last night of Hanukkah.   **Yes   No**

**Now show your answers to another student. Are your
answers the same or different? Why?**

**B. One word in each sentence is wrong. Find the word
and cross it out. Then write the correct word.**

1. Jewish families celebrate Hanukkah for ~~six~~ *eight* nights.
2. Another name for Hanukkah is the Festival of Songs.
3. On the third morning of Hanukkah, Jewish people light
    three candles.
4. Parents have fun playing traditional games.
5. Jewish families celebrate Hanukkah every summer.
6. Everybody eats special games, especially potato pancakes.

2 New Words

**Choose one of the following words or expressions to
complete each sentence. You can work with a classmate.**

applesauce   get together   ·   pancakes
hymn   Jewish   no wonder

1. The Festival of Lights is a _____*Jewish*_____ festival.
2. Jewish families _____ on eight nights to
    celebrate Hanukkah.
3. Families usually sing a _____ after the candle lighting
    ceremony.
4. People eat potato _____ at Hanukkah celebrations.
5. Cheese and _____ are also traditional foods for
    Hanukkah.
6. _____ Hanukkah is a happy time for children!

3 More Word Work

A. Find the words. Some words go across. Some words go down.

```
D L I G H T S G C A P H
E H A N U K K A H P A A
C Y P O T A T M E P N N
E M P A N C A E E L C U
M O L C H E E S S E A K
B G E (H Y M N) K E S K K
E K S O X L I G H A E A
M C A N D L E S K C I L
O C U M O N E G I F T S
N D C A K P O T A T O Y
E J E W I S H C A N D L
Y A V D E C E M B E R Z
```

Applesauce
Candles
Cheese
December
Games
Gifts
Hanukkah
Hymn
Jewish
Lights
Money
Pancake
Potato

B. Look at these words. Look for the synonyms of these words in the story "Hanukkah." Circle the synonyms. Then write the synonyms here.

1. celebration _*festival*_

2. evening _____

3. everyone _____

4. like _____

5. little _____

6. presents _____

7. too _____

4 Content Review

With a classmate, complete the sentences. Fill each blank with one word.

Eight nights every winter, Jewish people celebrate
Hanukkah . Families get together each night and light

_____. Then they usually eat potato _____

and applesauce. Children like this festival very much. They

_____traditional games. Their parents give them money and

small _____. Another name for Hanukkah is the Festival

of _____.

5 Discussion

What are the answers to these questions? Discuss your answers with another student.

1. What is another name for Hanukkah?
2. When is Hanukkah?
3. Who celebrates this festival?
4. What do people eat at Hanukkah celebrations?
5. How do children have fun at Hanukkah celebrations?
6. How many candles do Jewish people light on the sixth night of Hanukkah?
7. Why is Hanukkah a happy time for Jewish children?

6 Writing

A. Put these words in the right order.

1. _Children have fun playing games._

   games   fun   children   have   playing

2. _____

   money   parents   to   children   give

3. _____

   sing   candles   families   songs   and   light

4. _____

   families   eight   for   Hanukkah   Jewish   celebrate   nights

5. _____

   the   Lights   another   for   name   Hanukkah   is   of   Festival

B. Use these words in four original sentences.

get together   applesauce   hymn   candle

1. _____

2. _____

3. _____

4. _____

7 Think and Discuss

Think about these questions. Then discuss your ideas with the class.

Jewish people light candles to celebrate Hanukkah. Do people in the United States use candles for any other celebrations? In what celebrations do people in your country use candles?

CHRISTMAS

Find the month of December on a calendar.

What is the date of Christmas?

What do you see in the pictures?

Do you think this is a happy or sad day?

Learn these words with your teacher.

Christmas card	plant	wish
Christmas carol	ornament	wrap

Christmas

Christmas is one of the most popular holidays in the United States. Christmas Day is December 25, but preparations begin weeks before this date. During the days before Christmas, people buy gifts and send Christmas cards to friends and relatives. Many families decorate their homes with plants that are red and green, the traditional colors for Christmas. Families also buy a tree and decorate it with ornaments and lights. They wrap gifts with colored paper and put them under the Christmas tree. Parents tell small children that the gifts are from Santa Claus.

Christmas is a very happy time of the year. Streets and shop windows are beautiful with special lights and decorations. There are parties in schools and offices. People eat special foods: fruitcake, Christmas cookies, candies, and nuts. People wish each other "Merry Christmas," give gifts to their friends, and sing traditional songs called Christmas carols.

Families usually come together for the Christmas holiday. Christmas is the day most Americans celebrate the birth of Jesus Christ. On the night before Christmas, many families go to church. Many other families go to church on Christmas morning. When they return home, they open their gifts and then have a traditional Christmas dinner: turkey or ham, sweet potatoes, vegetables, cranberry sauce, and dessert.

1 Comprehension

A. Circle yes or no after each sentence.

1.	Christmas is a very popular holiday.	(Yes)	No
2.	People buy gifts on December 25.	Yes	No
3.	The colors for Christmas are green and red.	Yes	No
4.	Americans usually celebrate Christmas with their families.	Yes	No
5.	Many families go to church on December 25.	Yes	No
6.	Offices have parties to celebrate Christmas.	Yes	No
7.	People wrap trees with ornaments.	Yes	No

Now show your answers to another student. Are your answers the same or different? Why?

B. One word in each sentence is wrong. Find the word and cross it out. Then write the correct word.

happy

1. Christmas is a very ~~sad~~ time of the year.
2. Preparations for Christmas start years before December 25.
3. People send Christmas trees to their friends.
4. Families decorate their homes with green and white plants.
5. People have parties and wish Christmas carols.
6. Many families go to school on Christmas morning.

2 New Words

Choose one of the following words or groups of words to complete each sentence. You can work with a classmate.

plants	wrap	Christmas carols
decorate	ornaments	Christmas cards

1. People decorate Christmas trees with beautiful ___ornaments___ .

2. Many people sing _____ in church on December 25.

3. During the week before Christmas, many families _____ their homes with beautiful plants.

4. The _____ are green and red, the traditional Christmas colors.

5. People usually _____ Christmas gifts in pretty paper.

6. Many people send _____ to their friends and relatives in December.

3 More Word Work

A. Find the words. Some words go across. Some words go down.

```
C E S Y C L A G R E E N O P
O C A R D F R U I T C U D A
O A N U T D E C O R A T E O
K N T R E A D E C E M B E R
I D A C A N D Y A R G I F N
T K C O O K C H R E F S C A
R W L O W R A P O E R A H M
E Y A K S Q N U L N U N R E
E P U I R E D E C E I T I N
L Q S L F P L G I F T A S T
F R U I T C N U T S C C T C
A C H R I S T M A S A L M A
C O O K I E S A N T K O E R
S P G A W I S H Q L E L N O
```

Candy	Santa Clau[s]
Card	Tree
Carol	Wish
Christmas	Wrap
Cookies	
December	
Decorate	
Fruitcake	
Gift	
Green	
Nuts	
Ornament	
Red	

B. Circle the words that go with the celebration of Christmas in the United States.

parade   (green)   church   newspaper

gifts   shopping   beach   blue

tree   turkey   baseball ornaments

family   rain   red   bird

cards   music   picnic   fruitcake

4 Content Review

With a classmate, complete the sentences. Fill each blank with one word.

Christmas is a very happy time of the ____*year*____. Families

decorate trees with lights and _____. People sing traditional

songs called Christmas _____. People wrap gifts in

pretty paper and _____ them to their friends and relatives.

They _____ each other "Merry Christmas." Many families

go to _____ and then, at home, open their _____

and have a traditional Christmas dinner.

5 Discussion

What are the answers to these questions? Discuss your answers with another student.

1. What is the date of Christmas?
2. When do preparations for Christmas begin?
3. How do people celebrate in offices?
4. Why do people buy gifts in December?
5. What special foods do Americans eat at Christmas?
6. What is a Christmas tree?
7. What are Christmas cards?
8. When do people in your country give gifts to friends and relatives?
9. On what special day do you decorate your home with plants and flowers?

6 Writing

A. Write questions to these answers.

1. What ___*are the traditional colors for Christmas*___ ?
   The traditional colors for Christmas are green and red.
2. What _____ ?
   Christmas carols are traditional songs that people sing during the Christmas holiday.
3. Where _____ ?
   People usually put gifts under the Christmas tree.
4. When _____ ?
   Preparations for Christmas begin weeks before Christmas Day.
5. Where _____ ?
   Many families go to church on Christmas morning.
6. When _____ ?
   People send Christmas cards during the days before Christmas.

B. Use these words in original sentences.

wish   Christmas cards   gifts   wrap

_____

_____

_____

_____

_____

_____

7 Think and Discuss

Think about these questions. Then discuss your ideas with the class.

A. Red and green are colors for Christmas. What other holidays have special colors? Can you name the holidays and their colors?

B. On what other days do people give gifts in the United States?

We Wish You a Merry Christmas

We wish you a Merry Christmas
We wish you a Merry Christmas
We wish you a Merry Christmas
And a Happy New Year!

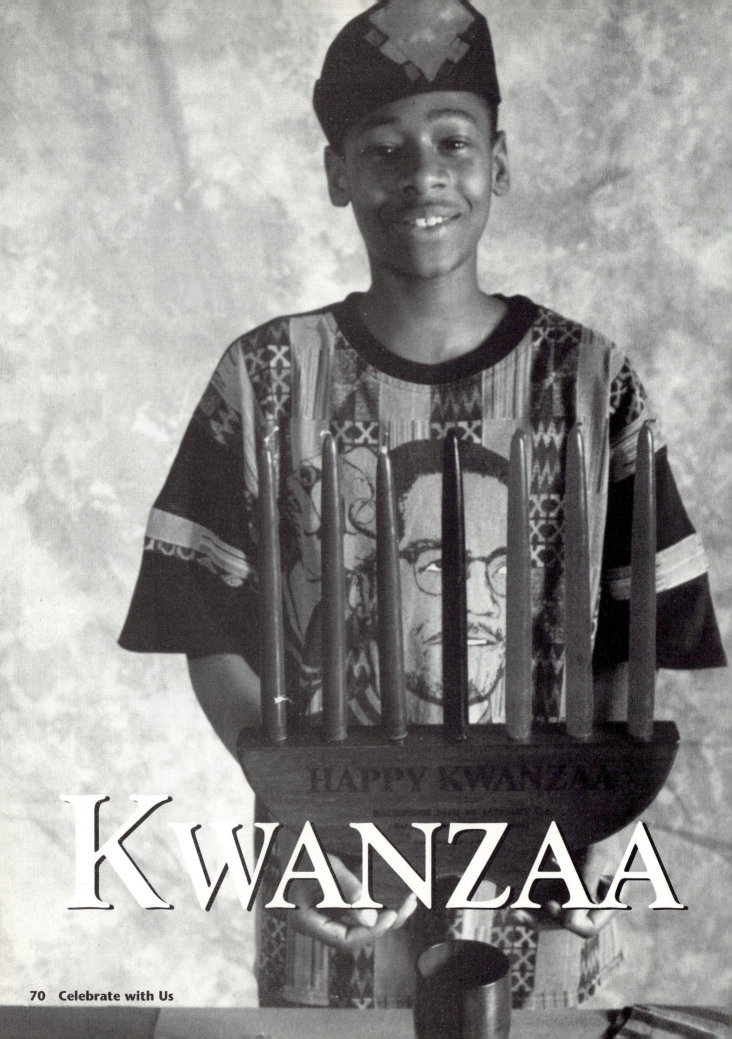

KWANZAA

What do you see in these pictures?

What is the girl doing?

Are these people happy or sad?

Learn these words with your teacher.

community	future	proud
culture	principle	set

Kwanzaa

In many homes in the United States, African-Americans celebrate a festival called Kwanzaa from December 26 to January 1. Kwanzaa is a celebration of the history and culture of black people in the United States. African-Americans are proud of their history and culture. As a result, Kwanzaa is a very happy festival.

A few days before the celebration, the family decorates the house. The decorations are black, red, and green—the traditional colors for Kwanzaa. The family sets a table with fruit, vegetables, and a candleholder with seven candles. The candles represent important principles of the African-American community.

Each night of Kwanzaa, a child lights a candle and then talks about the principle it represents. The biggest celebration is the evening of December 31. Friends, relatives, and neighbors get together in one home. Many people wear African clothes, children receive gifts, and there is a big dinner. After dinner, a party begins and everyone has fun singing songs and dancing.

Kwanzaa is an important festival for black Americans, especially children. At Kwanzaa time, they learn about their history, enjoy their culture, and think about their future.

1 Comprehension

A. Circle yes or no after each sentence.

1. Kwanzaa is an African-American celebration.   (Yes)   No
2. African-Americans celebrate Kwanzaa in December.   Yes   No
3. The colors for Kwanzaa are black, red, and blue.   Yes   No
4. Kwanzaa is a celebration of African-American history and culture.   Yes   No
5. People celebrate Kwanzaa for five days.   Yes   No

6. The biggest Kwanzaa celebration is
December 26.   **Yes**   **No**

7. Kwanzaa is a happy festival.   **Yes**   **No**

Now show your answers to another student. Are your answers the same or different? Why?

B. One word in each sentence is wrong. Find the word and cross it out. Then write the correct word.

1. Many African-Americans celebrate Kwanzaa from ~~November~~ *December* 26 to January 1.

2. The family decorates the house after the celebration.

3. The decorations are blue, red, and green.

4. Children light seven tables that represent important principles of their community.

5. The biggest Kwanzaa celebration is the morning of December 31.

6. Many people think African clothes and children receive gifts.

7. After a big dinner, people set songs and dance.

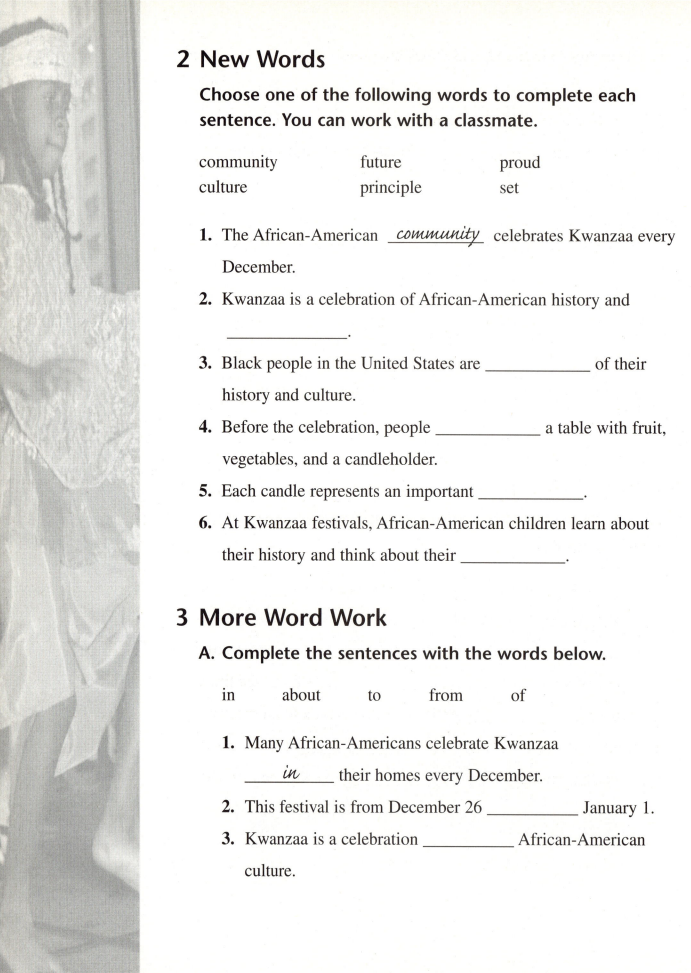

2 New Words

Choose one of the following words to complete each sentence. You can work with a classmate.

community   future   proud
culture   principle   set

1. The African-American _community_ celebrates Kwanzaa every December.

2. Kwanzaa is a celebration of African-American history and _____.

3. Black people in the United States are _____ of their history and culture.

4. Before the celebration, people _____ a table with fruit, vegetables, and a candleholder.

5. Each candle represents an important _____.

6. At Kwanzaa festivals, African-American children learn about their history and think about their _____.

3 More Word Work

A. Complete the sentences with the words below.

in   about   to   from   of

1. Many African-Americans celebrate Kwanzaa ____in____ their homes every December.

2. This festival is from December 26 _____ January 1.

3. Kwanzaa is a celebration _____ African-American culture.

4. Black people in the United States are proud _____ their

culture.

5. Friends and relatives get together _____ one house.

6. Children learn _____ African-American history at

Kwanzaa time.

B. Circle the words that you feel go with the celebration of Kwanzaa.

blue	five	December	vegetables
(fruit)	church	beach	bird
music	red	bus	culture
morning	candle	song	family
gift	picnic	black	newspaper
April	yellow	party	seven

4 Content Review

With a classmate, complete the sentences. Fill each blank with one word.

Every year, from December 26 to January 1,

African-American children light candles at Kwanzaa festivals.

_____ is a celebration of the _____ and culture

of black people in the United _____. At Kwanzaa time,

many people _____ African clothes and children receive

gifts. People talk about important _____ of the African-

American community. They also _____ songs and dance.

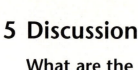

5 Discussion

What are the answers to these questions? Discuss your answers with another student.

1. What is Kwanzaa?
2. Who celebrates Kwanzaa?
3. When do people celebrate Kwanzaa?
4. What colors are Kwanzaa decorations?
5. How do people prepare their homes for Kwanzaa?
6. What happens on December 31?
7. Why is Kwanzaa important for African-American children?
8. Do people in your country have a festival like Kwanzaa?

6 Writing

A. Write questions to these answers.

1. When is _Kwanzaa_____?

   Kwanzaa is from December 26 to January 1.

2. Where _____?

   People celebrate Kwanzaa in their homes.

3. When _____?

   The family decorates the house a few days before

   the celebration.

4. What _____?

   Children receive gifts at Kwanzaa celebrations.

5. When _____?

   Everyone sings and dances after dinner.

B. Use these words in original sentences.

proud   future   culture   community

_____

_____

_____

_____

_____

_____

7 Think and Discuss

Think about these questions. Then discuss your ideas with the class.

A. People celebrate most holidays and festivals on one day. For example, Independence Day in the United States is July 4 and Halloween is October 31. African-Americans celebrate Kwanzaa for seven days. Do you know any other holidays or festivals that people celebrate for more than one day?

B. The principle for the first day of Kwanzaa is unity, especially unity in the family. Unity is staying together. Is unity in the family important? Why or why not?

NEW YEAR'S CELEBRATIONS

Look at a calendar. What is the first holiday of the year?

Where do you think these people are?

What are they doing?

Do you think they are happy or sad?

Learn these words with your teacher.

confetti	hug	resolution
habit	luck	whistle
horn	promise	

New Year's Celebrations

The beginning of the new year is a time for happy celebrations in the United States. The last day of the old year is New Year's Eve. This day is not a holiday, but at night many people go to parties at the homes of friends or in restaurants. New Year's Eve parties are lots of fun. People wear paper hats, eat, drink, and dance.

In New York City, thousands of people celebrate in the streets. At 11:59 P.M., people count the seconds until midnight. At midnight, people everywhere throw confetti and make noise with horns and whistles to welcome the new year. People kiss and hug their friends and family. They wish each other "Happy New Year" and then drink together to celebrate.

On New Year's Day, January 1, almost nobody works. Most people stay home and rest. Many people watch parades on television in the morning and football games in the afternoon. To have good luck in the New Year, people often eat special foods on New Year's Day. For example, in the South people eat black-eyed peas.

New Year's Day is a time to make promises for the new year. We call these promises resolutions. Many people want to stop bad habits in the new year. Some people say, "This year I will stop smoking." Others say, "I will work harder this year." But many people forget their resolutions already by January 2!

1 Comprehension

A. Circle yes or no after each sentence.

1.	New Year's Eve is December 31.	(Yes)	No
2.	People make noise at midnight to welcome the new year.	Yes	No
3.	Most people work on New Year's Day.	Yes	No
4.	New Year's Day is a time to make resolutions.	Yes	No
5.	There are parties in the morning of December 31.	Yes	No
6.	People wear paper hats at New Year's Eve parties.	Yes	No
7.	The first day of the year is New Year's Day.	Yes	No
8.	Many people watch football games on New Year's Eve.	Yes	No

Now show your answers to another student. Are your answers the same or different? Why?

B. One word in each sentence is wrong. Find the word and cross it out. Then write the correct word.

1. The last day of the old year is New Year's ~~Day~~. *Eve*
2. People wear paper horns at New Year's Eve parties.
3. At 11:59 P.M., people count the parades until midnight.
4. Everybody makes noise with confetti at midnight to celebrate the new year.
5. Most people stay home and work on New Year's Day.
6. Some people hug special foods to have good luck.
7. New Year's Day is a time to make whistles for the new year.
8. Many people want to start bad habits in the new year.

2 New Words

Choose one of the following words to complete each sentence. You can work with a classmate.

hug   luck   resolutions
confetti   whistles   habits

1. On New Year's Eve, people in the U.S.A. make noise and throw _confetti_ at midnight.

2. Many people make noise with _____ at New Year's Eve parties.

3. People often forget their _____ soon after New Year's Day.

4. On New Year's Day, people make promises to stop bad _____.

5. On New Year's Day, people in the South eat black-eyed peas for good _____ in the new year.

6. At midnight, people _____ their friends and wish them "Happy New Year."

3 More Word Work

Complete the puzzle on page 83.

Across

3. Many people watch ____ games on television.
6. New Year's Eve parties are usually at home or in a ____.
9. Many Americans ____ promises on New Year's Day.
11. At midnight, people ____ their friends.
12. Some people ____ special foods for good luck on New Year's Day.
13. At midnight, friends ____ each other "Happy New Year."
14. At 11:59, people begin to ____ the seconds until midnight.
16. On January 1, many people make promises to stop bad ____.

Down

1. People in the South eat black-eyed peas for ____ luck.
2. On December 31, many people go to parties to celebrate the new ____.
4. The beginning of a new year is always a ____ for celebration.
5. The first day of the year is New Year's ____.
6. New Year's Day is a time to make ____ for the new year.
7. Many people ____ at home on New Year's Day.
8. People ____ confetti at midnight to celebrate the new year.
10. People make noise with horns and ____ at midnight.
12. December 31 is New Year's ____.
15. Many people ____ paper hats at New Year's Eve parties.
17. On New Year's Day, many people stay home and watch ___.

4 Content Review

With a classmate, complete the sentences. Fill each blank with one word.

The beginning of the new ____*year*____ is a happy time in the _____ States. December 31 is not a _____, but at night there are many _____ in homes and restaurants. At midnight, people _____ noise with horns and whistles. They _____, hug, and wish each other "Happy _____ Year."

In New York City, people _____ in the streets. At 11:59, they _____ the seconds until midnight. Then everybody welcomes the _____ year with lots of noise.

5 Discussion

What are the answers to these questions? Discuss your answers with another student.

1. Where do many Americans celebrate the new year?
2. What do people do at midnight on December 31?
3. When is New Year's Day?
4. What is the date of New Year's Eve?
5. What happens in New York City on New Year's Eve?
6. Why do many people rest on New Year's Day?
7. What do some people do at home on New Year's Day?
8. When is New Year's Day in your country?
9. How do people celebrate New Year's Day in your country?
10. Do you make resolutions for the new year?
11. What special foods do you eat on New Year's Day?

6 Writing

A. Write five things that people do on New Year's Eve.

Example: *Many people go to parties.*

1. _____

2. _____

3. _____

4. _____

5. _____

Now write three things that people do on New Year's Day.

1. _____

2. _____

3. _____

Imagine that today is New Year's Day. You would like to stop some bad habits. Write three New Year's resolutions that you will make.

Example: *I will do all my homework every day.*

1. _____

2. _____

3. _____

B. Put the words in the correct order.

1. _People go to parties at night._

   parties   night   to   go   people   at

2. _____

   almost   New   Day   on   nobody   Year's   works

3. _____

   smoking   year   will   I   this   stop

4. _____

   to   want   people   habits   bad   stop

5. _____

   fun   New   of   lots   Eve   parties   are   Year's

7 Think and Discuss

Think about these questions. Then discuss your ideas with the class.

A. Some people have two new year's celebrations each year. They welcome the new year on January 1 and have another celebration on a different day. Do you know someone who celebrates New Year's Day twice each year? What do you know about the celebrations?

B. Imagine that you are an American. You want to stop three bad habits. What New Year's resolutions are you going to make?

Black-Eyed Peas

1 cup dried black-eyed peas
2 medium onions, chopped
1/2 teaspoon salt
1/4 teaspoon black pepper

Put peas and 3 cups of water in a bowl. Put the bowl in a refrigerator for 6 hours. Empty the water and put the peas in a pot. Add onions, salt, pepper, and 3 cups of water. Cover the pot and boil gently for one hour.

CHINESE NEW YEAR

Look at a map. Can you find China and Taiwan?

Do you have Chinese friends or classmates?

What do you see in the pictures?

What do you think these people are doing?

Learn these words with your teacher.

bill	envelope	lion
dragon	firecracker	explode

Chinese New Year

Chinese New Year is the most important holiday of the Chinese people. It begins when the new moon appears between the middle of January and the middle of February. Chinese and Chinese-American families have celebrations in many big cities in the United States. Before the celebration, people try to pay all their bills. Families clean their homes very well before the new year. Then they decorate their homes with flowers and fruit. They always have oranges because the orange is a symbol of good luck. Many other decorations are red because, in China, red is a happy color.

On the evening before Chinese New Year, families celebrate with a special dinner and gifts. Children receive money in bright red envelopes for good luck. Loud firecrackers explode at midnight to announce the new year.

New Year's Day is a very happy day in the Chinese community. Everyone wears new clothes to celebrate the beginning of a new year. The big event of the day is the parade in Chinatown. Several people wearing lion costumes dance in the parade. And there is always a group of men in the costume of a large dragon. During the parade, more noisy firecrackers explode. Happy Chinese New Year!

1 Comprehension

A. Circle <u>yes</u> or <u>no</u> after each sentence.

1. Chinese New Year is always in January.   Yes   No
2. Children receive red envelopes of money.   Yes   No
3. Chinese families clean their homes well
   after the parade.   Yes   No
4. The apple is a symbol of good luck.   Yes   No
5. There are Chinese New Year celebrations
   in many large American cities.   Yes   No

6. Families decorate their homes with fruit.　　　**Yes**　　　　**No**

7. The Chinese like to wear new clothes on
   New Year's Day.　　　　　　　　　　　**Yes**　　　　**No**

Now show your answers to another student. Are your answers the same or different? Why?

B. **One word in each sentence is wrong. Find the word and cross it out. Then write the correct word.**

1. Families decorate their ~~schools~~ *homes* well before the celebration of Chinese New Year.

2. They decorate their homes with flowers and costumes.

3. People try to pay all their bills after the new year.

4. Children receive money in red boxes for good luck.

5. Everyone wears new clothes to celebrate the end of a new year.

6. A group of men wear the costume of a large cat.

2 New Words

Choose one of the following words to complete each sentence. You can work with a classmate.

envelopes	explode	bills
lion	firecrackers	dragon

1. Chinese people do not want to have _____ *bills* _____ at the beginning of a new year.

2. They give children money in small red _____.

3. Firecrackers _____ at midnight to announce the new year.

4. Some people wear _____ costumes in the parade.

5. In the parade, there is a group of men wearing the costume of a large _____.

6. There are always loud and noisy _____ during the Chinese New Year parade.

3 More Word Work

A. Circle the words that you feel go with the celebration of Chinese New Year.

gifts	orange	church	parade
picnic	firecrackers	milk	food
blue	flowers	dragon	sun
umbrella	letter	coffee	bills
lion	potato	sad	fruit

B. Complete the puzzle on page 93.

Across

3. At midnight, loud _____ noises announce the new year.

8. On Chinese New Year's Day, a very popular event is the big _____.

9. Some people in the parade wear _____ costumes.

11. There is always a big _____ in a Chinese New Year's Day parade.

12. New Year's Day is the most important event in the _____ community.

Down

1. Children receive gifts of _____.

2. The orange is a symbol of good _____.

4. Parents give children money in small, _____ envelopes.

5. Before the New Year's celebrations, families _____ their homes very well.

6. Loud firecrackers _____ during the parade.

7. People want to pay all their bills before the new _____ begins.

10. People decorate their homes with fruit, especially _____.

4 Content Review

With a classmate, complete the sentences. Fill each blank with one word.

The most important festival of the ___Chinese___ people is the celebration of Chinese _____ Year. There are celebrations in many _____ in the United States. People wear _____ clothes to celebrate the new year. _____ receive gifts of money in small _____ envelopes. Families celebrate with a special _____. The popular event is always the _____ with noisy firecrackers and a large _____.

5 Discussion

What are the answers to these questions? Discuss your answers with another student.

1. When is Chinese New Year?
2. Do you know the date of Chinese New Year this year? What is it?
3. How do Chinese people prepare for the new year?
4. Why do Chinese people have oranges in their homes on New Year's Day?
5. What happens on the evening before Chinese New Year?
6. Why is the parade noisy?
7. When do people in your country decorate their homes with flowers?
8. Does your country have a festival like the celebration of Chinese New Year?
9. When do people give gifts of money in your country?
10. On what holiday do Americans use firecrackers?
11. When do people use firecrackers in your country?

6 Writing

Write four sentences about New Year's Day celebrations in your country. Then ask a classmate about the celebration of New Year's Day in his or her country. Write the information below.

My country is _____.

1. _____

2. _____

3. _____

4. _____

My classmate's country is _____.

1. _____

2. _____

3. _____

4. _____

What is the same about your celebrations?

_____

_____

7 Think and Discuss

Think about this question. Then discuss your ideas with the class.

Why do you think Chinese families clean their homes well and pay their bills before the beginning of the new year?

MARTIN LUTHER KING, JR., DAY

Who is the man in the picture?

Why is he famous?

Find the month of January on a calendar. What is the
date of Martin Luther King, Jr., Day?

Learn these words with your teacher.

equal rights	minister	speech
law	protest	peaceful
leader	restroom	

Martin Luther King, Jr., Day

Dr. Martin Luther King, Jr., was an important leader of black people and poor people in the U.S.A. When he was young, laws separated black people from white people. Black students and white students did not go to the same schools. Black people and white people did not eat in the same restaurants. They did not use the same theaters, hotels, or restrooms either.

Martin Luther King was a black minister of a church in Alabama. He did not like the laws that separated black people from white people. Dr. Martin Luther King wanted all people to have equal rights and live together in peace. He said, "Many people working together can change things." He led people in peaceful protests and marches. He also made speeches and wrote books about his ideas on equal rights and peaceful change.

After many marches and protests, Congress changed many laws to give equal rights to all people. Because of his work, Martin Luther King received the Nobel Peace Prize in 1964.

Some people were angry about the new laws. They did not want black people to have equal rights. In 1968, an angry man shot and killed Martin Luther King.

Martin Luther King's birthday is January 15. The third Monday in January is a national holiday honoring this great American leader. Many people today continue the work that Dr. King started. They are helping Americans live together in peace.

I Comprehension

A. Circle true or false after each sentence.

1. January 15 is Dr. Martin Luther King's birthday.   (True)   False

2. Martin Luther King wanted all Americans to live together in peace.   True   False

3. Martin Luther King wrote books about the Nobel Peace Prize.   True   False

4. A man killed Martin Luther King in 1964.   True   False

5. When Martin Luther King was young, black people and white people did not use the same restaurants.   True   False

6. Martin Luther King, Jr., Day is a national holiday.   True   False

Now show your answers to another student. Are your answers the same or different? Why?

B. One word in each sentence is wrong. Find the word and cross it out. Then write the correct word.

1. Dr. Martin Luther King was a leader of black people and ~~rich~~ *poor* people.

2. He was a black minister in a theater in Alabama.

3. Martin Luther King wanted everyone to have equal protests.

4. He made speeches and separated books about peaceful change.

5. Martin Luther King wrote the Nobel Peace Prize in 1964.

6. Many people continue the work that Martin Luther King stopped.

7. Martin Luther King's birthday is October 15.

2 New Words

Choose one of the words or the group of words below to complete each sentence. You can work with a classmate.

laws   leader   speeches
equal rights   minister   restrooms

1. When Martin Luther King was young, not all Americans

   had ___equal rights___ .

2. Black people and white people did not use the same _____.

3. Dr. King worked as a _____ in a church in Alabama.

4. He was also a famous _____ of black Americans.

5. Martin Luther King wanted Congress to change the

   _____ that separated black people from white people.

6. He wrote books and made _____ about equal rights.

3 More Word Work

A. Complete the puzzle.

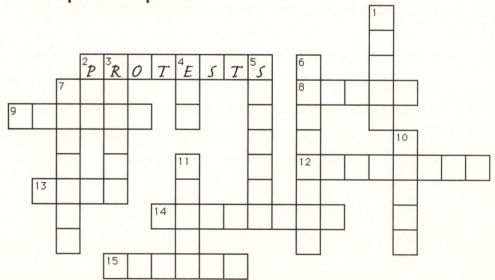

Across

2. Martin Luther King led peaceful marches and _____.

8. King wanted all Americans to live together in _____.

9. "Many people working together can _____ things."

12. _____ changed many laws to give everyone equal rights.

13. _____ separated black people from white people.

14. Martin Luther King was a famous _____ and leader.

15. Black people and white people did not use the same _____.

Down

1. When Martin Luther King was young, _____ people did not have equal rights.

3. King wanted all Americans to have equal _____.

4. When Martin Luther King was young, black people and white people did not _____ in the same restaurants.

5. Some people did not want black students and white students to study in the same _____.

6. Martin Luther King made many _____ about equal rights.

7. Martin Luther King, Jr., Day is _____ 15.

10. Martin Luther King received the Nobel Peace _____ in 1964.

11. Black people did not use the restrooms that _____ people used.

B. Look at these words. Look for the opposites of these words in the story "Martin Luther King, Jr., Day." Circle the opposites. Then write the opposites here. You should find two opposites for "old."

1. rich _____poor_____   **5.** different _____

2. happy _____   **6.** violent _____

3. few _____   **7.** stopped _____

4. old _____   **8.** gave _____

4 Content Review

With a classmate, complete the sentences. Fill each blank with one word.

Martin Luther King, Jr., was a ___minister___ of a church in Alabama. When he was young, _____ separated black people from white _____ in the United States. Martin Luther King did not like these laws. He wanted everyone to have equal _____. He wanted all people to live together in _____. Martin Luther King led people in peaceful _____ and made many speeches. He received the Nobel Peace _____ in 1964. The third Monday in _____ is a national holiday honoring this important American leader.

5 Discussion

What are the answers to these questions? Discuss your answers with another student.

1. Who was Dr. Martin Luther King, Jr.?
2. Did he have white classmates when he was young? Why?
3. Why did Martin Luther King write books?
4. Why did he receive the Nobel Peace Prize?
5. How did Martin Luther King die?
6. When do Americans remember and honor Martin Luther King?
7. What is the date of Martin Luther King, Jr., Day this year?
8. Who was an important leader in your country?
9. Does your country have a holiday for this person?

6 Writing

A. Put these words in the right order.

1. _Congress changed many laws._

many   Congress   changed   laws

2. _____

have   rights   not   equal   people   did   black

3. _____

a   Monday   January   holiday   is   in   the   third   national

4. _____

Luther   books   Martin   speeches   made   King   wrote   and

5. _____

peace   together   he   wanted   people   in   all   to   live

6. _____

many   happy   laws   were   about   the   very   new   people

B. Write three original sentences using the following words.

law   speech   leader

1. _____

2. _____

3. _____

7 Think and Discuss

Think about these questions. Then discuss your ideas with the class.

A. Dr. Martin Luther King, Jr., did not work in a hospital. Why do you think people call him <u>Dr.</u> Martin Luther King?

B. Imagine that Martin Luther King is living now. What would he say about Americans today?

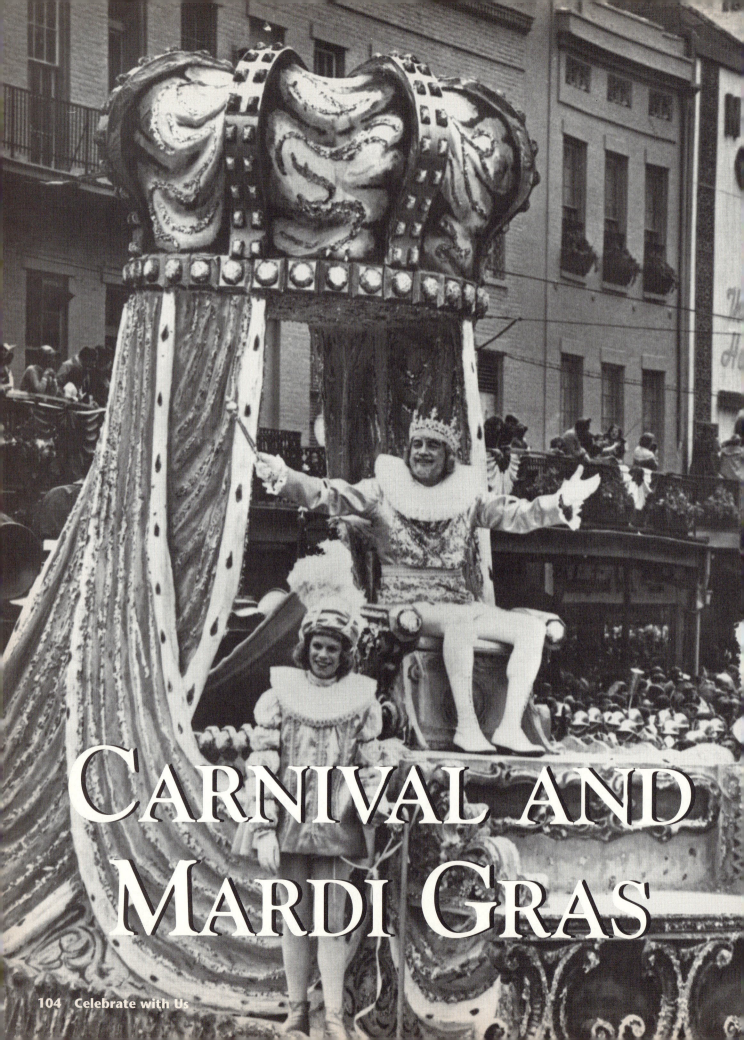

CARNIVAL AND MARDI GRAS

What do you see in the pictures?

What are these people wearing?

Do you like parades? Why or why not?

Can you find Louisiana on a map? Do you know anyone from Louisiana?

Now find France on a map. Do you know anyone from France?

Learn these words with your teacher.

ball	float	elegant	spicy
clown	jazz	full	

Carnival and Mardi Gras

Carnival is a festival full of music, parades, and costumes. There are Carnival celebrations in Brazil, Panama, Italy, and many other countries of the world. In the United States, Americans celebrate Carnival mainly in New Orleans, Louisiana. The festival begins there on January 6 and continues for a month or more.

During the first weeks of Carnival, many people go to elegant parties and balls. Then, during the last week of the festival, in February or March, the celebration does not stop. There are parties, balls, and about fifty different parades day and night. Beautiful floats pass by and marching bands play jazz music. Thousands of people dance in the streets.

Mardi Gras is the traditional name of the last day of Carnival. On this day, people wear costumes and masks in the streets. Men, women, and children dress as kings, queens, Native Americans, clowns, and even animals. Everyone watches the parades and dances until midnight.

A long time ago, Louisiana belonged to France. Immigrants from France brought the Carnival celebration to Louisiana over 200 years ago. In our times, visitors from many states and countries come to New Orleans every year for Carnival and Mardi Gras. Visitors enjoy the city's jazz bands, the typical drinks, and spicy foods. And they have lots of fun celebrating Carnival!

1 Comprehension

A. Circle true or false after each sentence.

1. People celebrate Carnival in many countries. **(True)** **False**

2. Americans celebrate Carnival in New Orleans. **True** **False**

3. Carnival is a very sad celebration. **True** **False**

4. Mardi Gras is in January. **True** **False**

5. People have fun in the streets during Carnival and Mardi Gras. **True** **False**

6. Beautiful floats dance in the streets during Carnival. **True** **False**

7. French immigrants brought Carnival to Louisiana. **True** **False**

8. There are many parades during Carnival celebrations. **True** **False**

9. Louisiana belonged to England a long time ago. **True** **False**

Now show your answers to another student. Are your answers the same or different? Why?

B. One word in each sentence is wrong. Find the word and cross it out. Then write the correct word.

1. Immigrants from ~~England~~ *France* brought Carnival to Louisiana over 200 years ago.

2. The festival starts in January and continues for a week.

3. Marching bands sing jazz music during Carnival in New Orleans.

4. The name of the first day of Carnival is Mardi Gras.

5. On Mardi Gras, people wear floats and masks.

6. Everyone has fun watching the parties and dancing in the streets.

7. Visitors come to New Orleans every month to celebrate Mardi Gras.

2 New Words

Choose one of the following words to complete each sentence. You can work with a classmate.

elegant   spicy   full   jazz
floats   balls   clowns

1. Some people wear very ___*elegant*___ costumes at Carnival balls.
2. There are always many large _____ in Mardi Gras parades.
3. The typical music of New Orleans is _____.
4. Many people dress as _____ during Mardi Gras celebrations.
5. During Mardi Gras, streets in New Orleans are _____ of people having fun.
6. Some typical foods in New Orleans are very _____.
7. Many people go to elegant parties and _____ to celebrate Mardi Gras.

3 More Word Work

A. Find the words. Some words go across. Some words go down.

```
Q C L O W N K A M U S I
I B O I M M I G R A N T
J K U B U A N C E L E A
A C A R N I V A L O W L
Z O S A S F L R E U P Y
Z S P Z F L O N G I A Z
I T I I K O F I A S R E
M U C L P A R V N I A M
M M Y D E T A C T A D U
I E T A L Y N K H N E S
G K I N G U C B R A Z I
R A M C O S E L E G A C
```

Brazil   Music
Carnival   Parade
Clown   Spicy
Costume
Elegant
Float
Immigrant
Italy
Jazz
King
Louisiana

B. Cross out the word that does not belong.

1. party   ball   ~~spicy~~   parade
2. band   clown   music   jazz
3. Italy   February   Brazil   Panama
4. parade   float   band   world
5. visitor   immigrant   Carnival   woman

4 Content Review

With a classmate, complete the sentences. Fill each blank with one word.

Carnival is a festival of ___*music*___, parades, and costumes. Americans celebrate _____ every year in New Orleans, Louisiana. The festival _____ in January and continues for a month or more.

The _____ day of Carnival is Mardi _____. This is the day people _____ masks and costumes in the streets. Everybody _____ fun watching the parades and dancing until _____.

Immigrants brought the carnival celebration from _____ to Louisiana over 200 years ago.

5 Discussion

What are the answers to these questions? Discuss your answers with another student.

1. In what countries do people celebrate Carnival?
2. Where do Americans celebrate Carnival?
3. When does the celebration begin?
4. What is Mardi Gras?
5. Who brought the Carnival festival to Louisiana?
6. How do people in New Orleans have fun during Carnival and Mardi Gras?
7. Does your country have a festival like Mardi Gras? When?
8. When do people wear masks in your country?

6 Writing

Put these words in the right order.

1. _Americans celebrate Carnival in New Orleans._____

   New   Americans   in   Orleans   Carnival   celebrate

2. _____

   Gras   is   in   Orleans   Mardi   a   New   festival

3. _____

   midnight   until   have   people   dancing   fun

4. _____

   people   wear   on   Mardi   costumes   Gras

5. _____

   to   visitors   Louisiana   to   come   Carnival   many   enjoy

7 Think and Discuss

Think about this question. Then discuss your ideas with the class.

People in New Orleans like to wear costumes and masks on Mardi Gras. Do you know any other occasions when Americans like to wear costumes or masks?

Valentine's Day

Look at the month of February on a calendar.
What is the date of Valentine's Day?

What do you see in the pictures?

Are these people happy or sad?

Learn these words with your teacher.

chocolate	heart	romantic
couple	message	sweetheart
friendship		

Valentine's Day

February 14 is a special day for sweethearts. It is Valentine's Day. It is a day for love and friendship.

On Valentine's Day, people send cards called valentines to their sweethearts, their friends, and members of their families. Almost all valentines have a red heart, the traditional symbol of love.

Some valentines are romantic. They have messages of love. Many valentines have the simple message, "Be my Valentine." This can mean, "Be my friend" or "Be my sweetheart."

Not all valentines are romantic. Many have funny messages and pictures. Children like to give funny valentines to their friends and classmates at school.

Valentine's Day is a happy time of the year. Sweethearts and married couples often give more than just romantic cards on Valentine's Day. They give gifts, too. Flowers and chocolate candy are very popular Valentine's Day gifts.

February 14 is a very special day of the year. On this day we say, "I love you."

1 Comprehension

A. Circle <u>true</u> or <u>false</u> after each sentence.

1. Valentine's Day is February 24.	True	(False)
2. On Valentine's Day, people send messages of love to their friends and sweethearts.	True	False
3. The blue heart is a symbol of love.	True	False
4. All valentines have messages of love.	True	False
5. Men give flowers to their sweethearts on Valentine's Day.	True	False
6. Most valentines have a red heart.	True	False

7. Valentines can be romantic or funny. **True   False**
8. Children like to give romantic valentines
   to their classmates. **True   False**

Now show your answers to another student. Are your answers the same or different? Why?

B. One word in each sentence is wrong. Find the word and cross it out. Then write the correct word.

1. People send cards called ~~sweethearts~~ *valentines* to their friends on Valentine's Day.
2. Almost all valentines have a red flower, a symbol of love.
3. Funny valentines have messages of love.
4. Chocolate candy and books are popular Valentine's Day gifts.
5. Children give sad valentines to their friends at school.

2 New Words

Choose one of the following words to complete each sentence. You can work with a classmate.

romantic	chocolate	friendship
messages	heart	couples

1. Some valentines are __*romantic*__ and others are funny.

2. Valentine's Day is usually a happy time for sweethearts and married _____.

3. Men often give _____ candy or flowers to their wives on Valentine's Day.

4. The red _____ is a symbol of love.

5. Many people send _____ of love to members of their families in February.

6. Valentine's Day is a special time for love and _____.

3 More Word Work

A. Circle the words that you feel go with the celebration of Valentine's Day.

(flowers)	gift	beach	romantic
card	love	church	blue
October	yellow	heart	sweetheart
friendship	doctor	picnic	girlfriend
red	sad	February	parade

B. Complete the sentences with the words below.

at   of   on   to

1. Valentine's Day is a happy time ____*of*____ the year.

2. Many people receive flowers _____ Valentine's Day.

3. The red heart is a symbol _____ love.

4. People send valentines _____ their friends _____ February 14.

5. Children give funny valentines _____ their friends _____ school.

4 Content Review

With a classmate, complete the sentences. Fill each blank with one word.

On February 14, people send cards called _valentines_ to their friends. Many valentines are _____. They have messages of love. Other _____ have very funny pictures and messages. _____ give funny valentines to their classmates at _____. Almost all valentines have a red _____, the traditional symbol of love. Chocolate _____ and flowers are popular Valentine's Day gifts.

5 Discussion

What are the answers to these questions? Discuss your answers with another student.

1. When is Valentine's Day?
2. What are valentines?
3. What does "Be my Valentine" mean?
4. What is a sweetheart?
5. What is the traditional symbol of love?
6. What gifts do many people receive on February 14?
7. Do you have a special day like Valentine's Day in your country? When is it?
8. How do people celebrate this day?
9. How are you going to celebrate Valentine's Day this year?

6 Writing

On Valentine's Day, many people put special messages in newspapers. Read these Valentine's Day messages. Then write two valentine messages: one for your sweetheart and one for a relative.

SUE
I LOVE YOU
ALWAYS & ALWAYS
BILL

SUZANNE
I love you more than any person, place or thing in the universe. You are my life, I love you.
BE MY VALENTINE
William

Jessica–I'm so happy you're my daughter. Always be my sweet Valentine.   I Love You. Daddy

SAM
Happy Valentine's Day to the love and light of my life. You hold the key to my heart forever.
LOVE, Cathy

PAUL
You are my Valentine,
Today, Tomorrow, Forever!
Love, LAURA

Maria–Happy Valentine's Day
With All My Love.
Your Loving Husband, R. J.

Allison Wright
Thank you Mother for your love, support, instruction & inspiration.
WE LOVE YOU! Jean & Tom

Linda, I love you now & I will love you forever.
Be my Valentine   Love Doug

HAPPY VALENTINE'S DAY TERESA

— To the world's greatest wife & mom. Love John, Pam, Patrick

1. _____

    _____

    _____

2. _____

    _____

    _____

7 Think and Discuss

Think about these questions. Then discuss your ideas with the class.

A. Valentine's Day is not always a happy time for everyone. How can Valentine's Day make someone sad?

B. What does "A friend in need is a friend indeed" mean?

PRESIDENTS' DAY

Who are the men in the pictures?

Why are they famous?

Where else can we see their pictures?

Learn these words with your teacher.

capital	penny	quarter
dollar bill	president	slave
independence		

Presidents' Day

Two famous American presidents were born in February. Abraham Lincoln was born on February 12. George Washington was born on February 22. We celebrate Presidents' Day on the third Monday in February. This day is between Lincoln's and Washington's birthdays. It is a national holiday and honors both presidents.

George Washington was a leader of the army that won independence for the United States from England. He became the first president of the United States. He chose the location for the nation's capital city. Americans call George Washington the "Father of his Country." We can see a picture of George Washington on the quarter and the one-dollar bill.

Abraham Lincoln was the sixteenth president of the United States. When he was president, eleven southern states left the United States and started a new country. There was a terrible war, but Lincoln made the United States one country again. He also freed the slaves. Abraham Lincoln's picture is on the penny and the five-dollar bill.

Washington and Lincoln were both great leaders in American history. On their day every February, Americans remember and honor these two great presidents.

1 Comprehension

A. Circle _true_ or _false_ after each sentence.

1. On Presidents' Day, Americans remember two famous presidents.   (True)   False

2. Abraham Lincoln was the first president of the United States.   True   False ✓

3. The one-dollar bill has a picture of George Washington.   True ✓   False

4. Abraham Lincoln freed the slaves.   True ✓   False

5. Abraham Lincoln's picture is on the quarter.   True   False ✓

6. Southern states started a new country when George Washington was president.   True   False ✓

7. George Washington chose the location for the capital of the United States.   True ✓   False

Now show your answers to another student. Are your answers the same or different? Why?

B. One word in each sentence is wrong. Find the word and cross it out. Then write the correct word.

1. Presidents' Day is a national holiday that honors ~~three~~ *two* presidents.
2. We celebrate Presidents' Day on the third Monday in March.
3. Abraham Washington was the first president of the United States.
4. Americans call him the "Father of his capital."
5. There is a picture of George Washington on the penny.
6. Abraham Lincoln made the United States one city again.
7. He also freed the states.
8. We can see a picture of Abraham Lincoln on the quarter.

2 New Words

Choose one of the words or the group of words below to complete each sentence. You can work with a classmate.

capital ✓   dollar bill ✓   president ✓   slaves ✓
penny ✓   quarter   independence ✓

1. George Washington was the first ___president___ of the United States.

2. The United States won its _____ from England over 200 years ago.

3. George Washington's picture is on the one-_____.

4. Is Abraham Lincoln's picture on the quarter or the _____?

5. Washington, D.C., is the _____ of the United States.

6. Abraham Lincoln freed the _____.

7. A picture of the first president is on the _____.

3 More Word Work

A. Find the words. Some words go across. Some words go down.

L	A	G	Q	U	A	R	A	G	E	N	F
I	F	E	B	R	U	A	R	Y	P	K	E
N	E	N	N	I	A	R	M	Q	U	A	B
C	P	E	N	F	E	B	Y	F	E	B	R
O	R	R	A	Q	S	L	A	V	E	S	U
L	E	A	P	R	E	S	I	D	E	N	T
N	S	L	E	A	D	E	R	S	I	D	K
I	N	D	E	P	E	N	D	E	N	C	E
M	D	S	L	A	V	F	W	A	R	U	L
O	E	P	E	N	N	Y	E	V	L	P	E
P	Q	U	A	R	T	E	R	P	E	N	A
W	A	S	H	I	N	G	T	O	N	K	D

Army
February
Independence
Leaders
Lincoln
Penny
President
Quarter
Slaves
War
Washington

B. Circle the words that you feel go with the story of George Washington.

(February)	war	July	slaves
president	dime	France	blue
neighbor	China	quarter	famous
December	flower	train	penny
capital	leader	independence	church

Now copy the words that you feel go with the story of Abraham Lincoln.

_____

_____

4 Content Review

With a classmate, complete the sentences. Fill each blank with one word.

The third Monday in February is ___Presidents'___ Day. This national holiday honors George _____ and Abraham Lincoln. George Washington was the first _____ of the United States. A picture of George Washington is on the _____. Abraham Lincoln was the sixteenth president. He _____ the slaves. His picture is on the five-dollar _____. Washington and Lincoln were important leaders in _____ history.

5 Discussion

What are the answers to these questions? Discuss your answers with another student.

1. When is Presidents' Day?
2. What is the date of Presidents' Day this year?
3. Who do Americans remember on Presidents' Day?
4. Why is George Washington famous?
5. When is his birthday?
6. Why is Abraham Lincoln famous?
7. When is his birthday?
8. Whose picture can we see on a quarter?
9. Where can we see a picture of Abraham Lincoln?
10. Who is the president of the United States now?
11. Does your country have a holiday like Presidents' Day?
12. Who was a famous leader in your country's history?

6 Writing

A. Every country has a famous leader. Read this story.

Simon Bolivar

Simon Bolivar was an important leader in South America. He was born in Caracas, Venezuela, in 1783. He studied in Europe. He was a very important leader of an army in the war for the independence of South America. He was also a president. Simon Bolivar is very famous.

Now write a short story about a famous leader in your country.

_____

_____

_____

_____

B. Write the questions to these answers.

1. Who *was George Washington* _____?

   He was the first president of the United States.

2. When _____?

   His birthday is February 22.

3. Who _____?

   Abraham Lincoln freed the slaves.

4. When _____?

   He was born on February 12.

5. Where _____?

   We can see a picture of George Washington on the

   one-dollar bill.

6. When _____?

   It is the third Monday in February.

7 Think and Discuss

Think about these questions. Then discuss your ideas with the class.

A. Why do Americans call George Washington the "Father of his Country"?

B. The names Washington and Lincoln are very common in the United States. There are many places in this country that have these names. Do you know any places called Washington or Lincoln?

SAINT PATRICK'S DAY

Look at the month of March on a calendar. What is the
date of Saint Patrick's Day?

Find Ireland on a map. Is it near or far from the United States?

What do you see in the pictures?

What are the people doing?

Learn these words with your teacher.

Ireland	hero	shamrock
Irish	priest	boiled

Saint Patrick's Day

Saint Patrick is a very famous and important hero of Ireland. He was a priest in that country many years ago. Saint Patrick is famous because he built many churches for the Irish people.

Saint Patrick's Day is March 17. This day is a very important national holiday in Ireland. Immigrants from Ireland brought the celebration to the United States many years ago. In the United States, Saint Patrick's Day is especially popular in cities where there are many Irish-Americans. It is not a national holiday, but there are big celebrations in New York, Boston, Chicago, and many other cities and towns, too.

On Saint Patrick's Day, many people wear something green, the traditional color of Ireland. Some people wear a shamrock. The shamrock is a small green plant with three leaves. It is the national flower of Ireland. The shamrock is also a symbol of Saint Patrick's Day.

People work on Saint Patrick's Day, but they have fun, too. Radio stations play Irish music, many cities have big parades, and some people have parties in the evening. Celebrations often include a typical Irish dinner: boiled beef, cabbage, and potatoes. At first, only Irish and Irish-Americans celebrated Saint Patrick's Day. Now we say, "Everyone is Irish on Saint Patrick's Day."

1 Comprehension

A. Circle true or false after each sentence.

1. There are parades in many cities on Saint Patrick's Day.   (True)   False
2. Saint Patrick was a priest in Ireland.   True   False
3. On March 17, people wear something red.   True   False
4. Saint Patrick built shamrocks in Ireland.   True   False
5. People in the United States do not work on March 17.   True   False
6. Saint Patrick's Day is popular in Boston.   True   False

7. Radio stations play Irish music on
   Saint Patrick's Day.   **True   False**
8. The shamrock is a hero of Ireland.   **True   False**

**Now show your answers to another student. Are your
answers the same or different? Why?**

**B. One word in each sentence is wrong. Find the word
and cross it out. Then write the correct word.**

1. Saint Patrick was a ~~student~~ *priest* in Ireland.
2. Saint Patrick built many schools in Ireland.
3. May 17 is a very important national holiday in Ireland.
4. Many people wear something blue on Saint Patrick's Day.
5. The cabbage is the national flower of Ireland.
6. The shamrock is a small plant with five leaves.
7. Radio stations wear Irish music, and people have parties in
   the evening.
8. Celebrations often include a typical Irish dinner: boiled beef,
   shamrocks, and potatoes.

2 New Words

**Choose one of the following words to complete each
sentence. You can work with a classmate.**

Irish   hero   priest
shamrock   Ireland   boiled

1. The green _shamrock_ is a symbol of Saint Patrick's Day.
2. _____ music is very popular on Saint Patrick's Day.
3. Green is the traditional color of _____.
4. Saint Patrick is a famous _____ of Ireland.
5. Many people eat _____ beef and cabbage on March 17.
6. Saint Patrick was a _____ who built many churches in
   Ireland.

3 More Word Work

A. Find the words. Some words go across. Some words go down.

```
B I R E L P A R A D S        Beef
E R A C K V P L E V H        Cabbage
F E S H A M R O C K A        Green
O L G R P R I E S I M        Ireland
C A R I K B E F Q R G        Irish
A N E S M U S I C I R        Music
B D E T O D T J P S E        Parade
Y M N I (B E E F) N H D      Priest
S U P A R A D E H T K        Shamrock
H S T N C A B B A G E
G R E I R E L A M U S
```

B. Talk to classmates from five different countries. Ask for the name of their country and their nationality. Write the information on the lines below.

	Country	Nationality
1.	*Ireland*	*Irish*
2.		
3.		
4.		
5.		
6.		

4 Content Review

With a classmate, complete the sentences. Fill each blank with one word.

Many years ago, Saint Patrick was a ____*priest*____ in Ireland. Saint Patrick is an important _____ of Ireland because he built many _____ for the Irish people.

Saint Patrick's _____ is March 17. Many people like to _____ something green on Saint Patrick's Day. _____ stations play Irish music, and many cities have _____ to celebrate this day.

5 Discussion

What are the answers to these questions? Discuss your answers with another student.

1. Who is Saint Patrick?
2. Why is he famous?
3. When is Saint Patrick's Day?
4. Why is Saint Patrick's Day popular in New York City?
5. Why do people wear a shamrock on March 17?
6. How do Americans have fun on Saint Patrick's Day?
7. Do you wear green clothes often? What is your favorite color?
8. Who is an important hero in your country?
9. Does your country have a special day to remember this hero? When?
10. What is the national flower of your country?

6 Writing

A. Ask four classmates about what foods people usually eat for dinner in their countries. Write the name of each country and the food that people eat in a typical dinner there.

	Country	Dinner
1.	*Ireland*	*boiled beef, cabbage, potatoes*
2.		
3.		
4.		
5.		

B. Write the questions to these answers.

1. Who *is an important hero of Ireland* ?

   Saint Patrick is.

2. What _____ ?

   The shamrock is.

3. What _____ ?

   It is a small green plant with three leaves.

4. Why _____ ?

   He is famous because he built many churches in Ireland.

5. What _____ ?

   They play Irish music.

6. Where _____ ?

   There are big celebrations in New York, Boston, and Chicago.

7 Think and Discuss

Think about these questions. Then discuss your ideas with the class.

A. Why do people say, "Everyone is Irish on Saint Patrick's Day"?

B. Why do many people who are not Irish-Americans wear green on Saint Patrick's Day?

C. Irish immigrants brought the celebration of Saint Patrick's Day to the United States. What other popular celebrations did immigrants bring to this country?

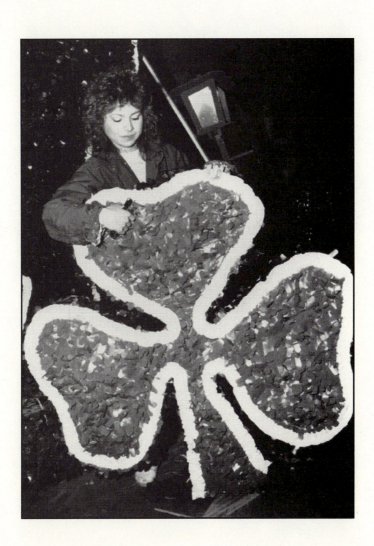

THE CHERRY BLOSSOM FESTIVAL

Look at a map. Can you find Japan?

Do you have any Japanese friends or classmates?

What do you see in the pictures?

Learn these words with your teacher.

blossom	photograph	annual
photography	cherry	tourist

The Cherry Blossom Festival

Spring is a beautiful time of the year in Washington, D.C. It is the time of the city's annual Cherry Blossom Festival. Cherry blossoms are the flowers of cherry trees. For ten days in March or April, millions of pretty pink and white flowers appear on about 3,000 cherry trees in our nation's capital.

Every spring, thousands of tourists come to Washington, D.C., to see the cherry blossoms and enjoy the Cherry Blossom Festival. During one week, there are special concerts, a beautiful parade, and an elegant dance. Photography is a very popular activity during the festival. Many people take photographs of their friends and relatives under the pretty cherry trees.

The cherry trees in Washington, D.C., are a gift from the people of Japan. The first trees came from Tokyo in 1912. They are a symbol of friendship between Japan and the United States. Their blossoms make our nation's capital very beautiful every spring.

1 Comprehension

A. Circle true or false after each sentence.

1. The Cherry Blossom Festival is in the spring. **(True)** **False**

2. Tourists come to Washington, D.C., in May to see the cherry blossoms. **True** **False**

3. The blossoms appear in March or April. **True** **False**

4. The cherry trees in Washington, D.C., are from Japan. **True** **False**

5. Every year, thousands of tourists buy beautiful cherry blossoms in Washington, D.C. **True** **False**

6. Many people take photographs of their families under the cherry trees. **True** **False**

7. There are concerts during the Cherry
   Blossom Festival.   **True**   **False**
8. Cherry blossoms are red and white flowers.   **True**   **False**

Now show your answers to another student. Are your answers the same or different? Why?

B. One word in each sentence is wrong. Find the word and cross it out. Then write the correct word.

blossoms
1. Millions of ~~birds~~ appear on cherry trees in Washington in March or April.
2. Cherry blossoms are the fruit of cherry trees.
3. Thousands of tourists come to Washington, D.C., in the summer to enjoy the Cherry Blossom Festival.
4. Many people bring photographs of their friends under the cherry trees.
5. The cherry festivals in Washington, D.C., are a gift from Japan.
6. The Japanese cherry trees in Washington, D.C., are a symbol of parades between Japan and the United States.
7. Cherry blossoms make our nation's concert very pretty every spring.

2 New Words

Choose one of the following words to complete each sentence. You can work with a classmate.

annual	blossoms	cherry
photography	tourists	photographs

1. The first ___*cherry*___ trees came to Washington from Japan in 1912.

2. Many _____ like to take photographs of their families under the cherry trees.

3. Many cherry trees have pink _____ in the spring.

4. Every spring, many people enjoy the _____ Cherry Blossom Festival in Washington, D.C.

5. Tourists like to take _____ of their friends under the cherry blossoms.

6. _____ is very popular during the Cherry Blossom Festival.

3 More Word Work

A. Circle the words that you feel go with the celebration of the Cherry Blossom Festival.

flowers	gift	orange	parade
France	pink	concert	summer
capital	bird	church	photography
picnic	spring	Brazil	tree
blue	Japan	tourist	friendship

B. Complete the sentences with the words below.

in   of   to   from

1. There are about 3,000 Japanese cherry trees _____*in*_____ Washington, D.C.

2. Tourists come _____ Washington, D.C., every year to see the cherry blossoms.

3. They take photos _____ their friends and relatives under the trees.

4. The first Japanese cherry trees in Washington came _____ Japan in 1912.

5. They are a gift from the people _____ Japan.

6. The cherry trees are a symbol _____ friendship between two countries.

4 Content Review

With a classmate, complete the sentences. Fill each blank with one word.

Every spring, thousands of _____*tourists*_____ come to Washington, D.C., to enjoy the city's _____ Blossom Festival. Cherry blossoms are the _____ of cherry trees. Pretty cherry blossoms _____ on about 3,000 trees every March or _____. Washington's cherry trees are a gift from _____. These beautiful trees are a symbol of _____ between Japan and the United States. Their _____ make Washington, D.C., very beautiful every spring.

5 Discussion

What are the answers to these questions? Discuss your answers with another student.

1. Why do many tourists come to Washington, D.C., in the spring?
2. How many cherry trees are there in Washington, D.C.?
3. Where are Washington's cherry trees from?
4. What are blossoms?
5. What color are cherry blossoms?
6. When do they appear?
7. What do people do during the Cherry Blossom Festival?
8. When did the people of Japan give the first cherry trees to the United States?
9. What is the name of the capital of Japan?
10. What is the capital of your country?
11. Do people in your country celebrate spring with a festival? What is the name of the festival?
12. What is your favorite flower? What color is it?

6 Writing

Write three sentences about the Cherry Blossom Festival. Look back at the story if you need help.

1. _____
2. _____
3. _____

Now write four or five sentences about a festival in your country.

1. _____

2. _____

3. _____

4. _____

5. _____

7 Think and Discuss

Think about these questions. Then discuss your ideas with the class.

A. Why are trees important for us? How do people use trees?

B. What are some of the main reasons that tourists visit Washington, D.C.?

C. Does your country have a gift from another country? What is it?

EASTER

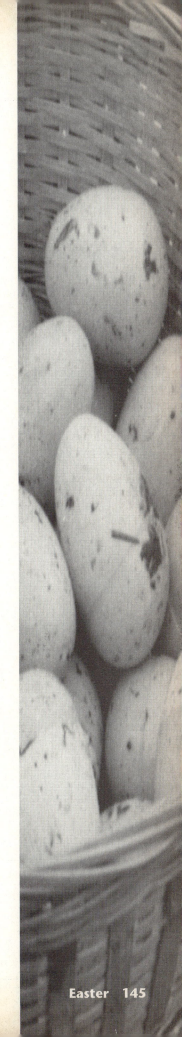

What do you see in the pictures?

What are the boys carrying?

What does the girl have in her hand?

Do you think they are happy or sad?

Learn these words with your teacher.

basket	happiness	nature
bunny	lily, lilies	

Easter

Easter is a very happy celebration. It is always on a Sunday in March or April. At this time of the year, people are glad that the cold days of winter are over. Spring is beginning, and there is new life in nature. People enjoy hearing birds sing again. People are happy to see pretty flowers and green leaves again.

Easter Sunday is not a national holiday, but it is a day of much happiness in churches. Beautiful white lilies decorate most churches, and celebrations often begin very early in the morning. Since Easter is a happy occasion, people like to wear new clothes. Because Easter is a very religious day, radio stations play religious music, and there are usually religious movies on television.

Easter is a special day for children. They color eggs and put them in pretty baskets. Children receive gifts of candy that they can put in their baskets, too. Parents tell their small children that the baskets of eggs and candy are gifts from the Easter Bunny.

Adults enjoy Easter, too. Many people give candy to their friends and relatives on Easter. Since Easter is in the spring, many people give flowers also. In the afternoon, families have a traditional Easter dinner: ham, vegetables, and dessert.

Easter is a very beautiful celebration. It is at the beginning of spring, when there is new life in plants and animals. Easter eggs and pretty flowers are symbols of this new life.

1 Comprehension

A. Circle _true_ or _false_ after each sentence.

1. Easter is always on Sunday.   (True)   **False**
2. Easter is a religious holiday.   **True**   **False**
3. Children have baskets with eggs and candy
   on Easter.   **True**   **False**
4. Easter is in April or May.   **True**   **False**
5. Many people like to wear new clothes on
   Easter Sunday.   **True**   **False**
6. There are red flowers in most churches on
   Easter Sunday.   **True**   **False**
7. People give flowers to friends on Easter.   **True**   **False**
8. The Easter Bunny is a gift for children.   **True**   **False**
9. People celebrate Easter at the beginning
   of summer.   **True**   **False**

Now show your answers to another student. Are your answers the same or different? Why?

B. One word in each sentence is wrong. Find the word and cross it out. Then write the correct word.

1. Easter is a ~~national~~ *religious* holiday.
2. Many celebrations in churches begin early in the evening on Easter Sunday.
3. People like to wash new clothes on Easter.
4. Children color birds and put them in baskets.
5. Easter is at the beginning of winter, when there is new life in nature.
6. Easter eggs and pretty children are symbols of this new life.

2 New Words

Choose one of the following words to complete each sentence. You can work with a classmate.

nature   bunny   baskets

happiness   lily

1. Small children think that their baskets of eggs are gifts from the

    Easter _____*Bunny*_____ .

2. Parents usually help children color the eggs for their Easter

    _____.

3. Easter Sunday is a day of much _____ in churches.

4. There is new life in _____ in the beginning of spring.

5. The _____ is the traditional flower for Easter.

3 More Word Work

A. Complete the puzzle.

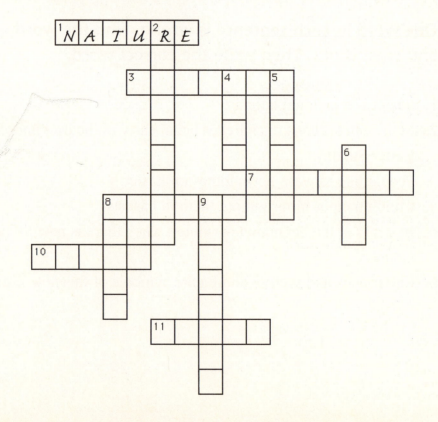

Across

1. In the spring, there is new life in ____.
3. People often give ____ to relatives on Easter.
7. Children usually have eggs and candy in their Easter ____.
8. On Easter Sunday, many people go to ____ early in the morning.
10. Children think that the Easter ____ leaves baskets of eggs for them on Easter Sunday.
11. Sometimes Easter is in ____ and sometimes it is in April.

Down

2. Easter and Christmas are ____ holidays.
4. Children like to color ____ for their Easter baskets.
5. Easter is always on a ____. It is never on a Tuesday.
6. People like to ____ new clothes on Easter Sunday.
8. Relatives often give children ____ to put in their baskets.
9. Small ____ usually have pretty baskets with eggs for Easter.

B. Circle four words that you feel go with the word "nature."

birds	plants	spring
year	candy	March
celebration	morning	movie
gift	basket	leaves
eggs	music	dessert

C. Now draw a line under four words that you feel go with the word "time."

D. In the story about Easter, find three more words that go with "nature" and three more words that go with "time." Write the words on the lines below.

Nature	Time
lilies	_Sunday_
_____	_____
_____	_____
_____	_____

4 Content Review

With a classmate, complete the sentences. Fill each blank with one word.

Easter is a very religious holiday in March or __April__. On Easter Sunday, many people go to _____ early in the morning. Easter is the day that children color _____ for their Easter baskets. Adults give candy or _____ to their friends and relatives. Many radio stations play _____ music. Everyone likes to wear new _____ on Easter Sunday because it is a very happy holiday.

5 Discussion

What are the answers to these questions? Discuss your answers with another student.

1. When do people celebrate Easter in the United States?
2. What is the date of Easter this year?
3. How do children celebrate Easter?
4. What gifts do adults receive on this holiday?
5. Is Easter a happy or sad occasion?

6. What do many people have for dinner on Easter Sunday?
7. What kind of music do radio stations play on Easter Sunday?
8. What are some examples of new life in nature?
9. What do many people do on Easter morning?
10. Does your country have a holiday like Easter?
11. When do people in your country give gifts of flowers?
12. Do people in your country color eggs? When?

6 Writing

Many people like spring. Other people like summer or fall or winter. What is your favorite season? Write a few sentences about your favorite season. Here is an example:

I like summer. I usually have my vacation in the summer. The days are very hot, and I go swimming a lot. Sometimes I go to the beach with my friends. Sometimes we have picnics in a park. Summer is my favorite season.

Now write your sentences below.

_____

_____

_____

_____

7 Think and Discuss

Think about these questions. Then discuss your ideas with the class.

Are eggs and flowers good symbols of new life in nature? Why or why not?

CINCO DE MAYO

Find Mexico on a map. Is Mexico near or far from the United States?

Look at a map of the United States. Can you find Arizona, New Mexico, and California? Are they near or far from Mexico?

What do you see in the pictures?

What do you think these people are doing?

Learn these words with your teacher.

battle	vendor	southwestern
region	victory	fireworks

Cinco de Mayo

Cinco de Mayo is a Mexican holiday. It is also a very special day in most of California and the southwestern part of the United States. This region of the country was once part of Mexico, and now many Mexican-Americans live there. Cinco de Mayo means the fifth of May in Spanish. On May 5, 1862, Mexican soldiers won a famous battle against the French army in the city of Puebla, Mexico. Every year, Mexicans and Mexican-Americans celebrate this victory.

Cinco de Mayo is always a very happy occasion. It is a day to celebrate with the Mexicans and Mexican-Americans in the United States. The special colors of the day are green, red, and white—the colors of the Mexican flag. Cities and towns have many exciting activities on this day. There is usually a big parade with bands playing Mexican music. Many adults and children wear beautiful Mexican clothes.

After the parade, people usually enjoy other festivities in a large park. Here vendors sell Mexican foods and drinks, and there is a program of Mexican songs and dances. The evening ends with a beautiful show of bright fireworks.

1 Comprehension

A. Circle true or false after each sentence.

1. Cinco de Mayo is a day of parades, music, and fireworks. **True** False
2. Many Mexican-Americans live in California. **True** **False**
3. Most people celebrate Cinco de Mayo at the beach. **True** **False**
4. Cinco de Mayo celebrates the French army. **True** **False**
5. Cinco de Mayo is the fifth of May. **True** **False**
6. The flag of Mexico is green, white, and red. **True** **False**
7. The festivities begin with a show of fireworks. **True** **False**

Now show your answers to another student. Are your answers the same or different? Why?

B. One word in each sentence is wrong. Find the word and cross it out. Then write the correct word.

1. Cinco de Mayo is a ~~French~~ *Mexican* holiday.
2. It is also a special day in California and the northern region of the United States.
3. The special colors for this celebration are the colors of the Mexican flag: red, white, and blue.
4. There is a parade with bands that dance Mexican music.
5. Many people celebrate pretty Mexican clothes.
6. Vendors buy Mexican foods and drinks.
7. The southwestern region of the United States was once part of France.

2 New Words

Choose one of the following words to complete each sentence. You can work with a classmate.

battle   southwestern   victory
region   vendors   fireworks

1. People buy Mexican drinks from ____*vendors*____ during the festivities.

2. Cinco de Mayo is a celebration of the _____ of Mexican soldiers over the French army in 1862.

3. Many Mexican-Americans live in the southwestern _____ of the United States.

4. There was an important _____ between France and Mexico in 1862.

5. Arizona and New Mexico are _____ states.

6. The festivities end with _____ at night.

3 More Word Work

A. Find the words. Some words go across. Some words go down.

```
M U S I C F V I C T D S
E S O L D I E R S E C O
X C U K O R N S V K A L
B A T T L E D O I B L D
A L H U I W O N C P I I
T I W O N O R G T A F E
T F E Y C R E S O R O V
V O S O U K Y L R A R E
E R T H K S M A Y D F N
Q N E S O U T H W E I D
D I R E G I O N A R M Y
O A N S O M E X I C O K
```

Army
Battle
California
Fireworks
May
Mexico
Music
Parade
Region
Songs
Southwestern
Vendor
Victory

B. Cross out the word that does not belong.

1. battle	soldier	~~vendor~~	army
2. food	dance	song	music
3. festivity	holiday	celebrate	southwestern
4. parade	program	show	region
5. vendor	victory	drink	food

4 Content Review

With a classmate, complete the sentences. Fill each blank with one word.

The Cinco de Mayo festival is very popular in the

southwestern region of the United States. This region was

once part of _____. During the festival, bands in parades

_____ Mexican music. Many children and adults

_____ Mexican clothes. After the parade, people enjoy

other activities in a _____. They buy Mexican foods and

drinks from _____. The festivities usually end with a show

of _____ in the evening.

5 Discussion

What are the answers to these questions? Discuss your answers with another student.

1. When is the Cinco de Mayo celebration?
2. What do people celebrate on this day?
3. What states are in the southwestern region of the United States?
4. Why are green, white, and red the special colors of Cinco de Mayo?
5. Does the city where you live celebrate Cinco de Mayo? Why or why not?
6. Do people celebrate Cinco de Mayo only in the United States?
7. Do people in your country use fireworks? When?
8. Do you like Mexican food?
9. What other kinds of food do you like?

6 Writing

A. Put these words in the right order.

1. _Many Mexican-Americans live in California._

   in   many   live   California   Mexican-Americans

2. _____

   parades   cities   have   fifth   on   May   many

3. _____

   music   Mexican   play   bands   in   parades

4. _____

   activities   large   in   there   a   are   many   park

5. _____

   dances   songs   Mexican   and   enjoy   people

6. _____

   with   fireworks   festivities   show   end   the   a   of

B. Write questions to these answers.

1. What _does Cinco de Mayo mean_____?

   It means May fifth.

2. What _____?

   It is green, red, and white.

3. Where _____?

   They live in the southwestern part of the United States.

4. When _____?

   They won the battle on May 5, 1862.

5. What _____?

   Many children wear beautiful Mexican clothes.

7 Think and Discuss

Think about these questions. Then discuss your ideas with the class.

A. Some holidays are times for parades. When are there parades in the city where you live? When are there parades in your country? Why do people like parades?

B. California once belonged to Mexico. Do you know what country Louisiana once belonged to? What can you say about New York, Alaska, and Texas?

MOTHER'S DAY AND FATHER'S DAY

Look at the month of May on a calendar. When is Mother's Day?

What do you see in the pictures?

Are these people happy or sad?

Learn these words with your teacher.

brunch	florist	tray
business	parent	express
corsage	relaxation	

Mother's Day and Father's Day

The second Sunday in May is Mother's Day. This is the day people show their love for their mothers. Sons and daughters express their love with cards and gifts. People who live far away call their mothers on the telephone to wish them a "Happy Mother's Day."

Mother does not work on Mother's Day. She enjoys a day of rest with her family. In some homes, her husband and children serve her breakfast on a tray in bed. In many homes, they prepare dinner for her also. Other families have brunch or dinner in a restaurant to honor their mothers and grandmothers.

Flowers are an important part of Mother's Day. Mothers and grandmothers often receive flowers, a pretty plant, or a beautiful corsage for the celebration. In fact, florists do a lot of business during the days before Mother's Day.

Fathers have a special day, too. People show love for their fathers on Father's Day, the third Sunday in June. This holiday is a day of relaxation for fathers and grandfathers. They receive cards and presents. They have their favorite foods for dinner.

Mothers and fathers are very important people. They work hard all year to help their families. Mother's Day and Father's Day are times to give special thanks to parents for all their hard work and love.

1 Comprehension

A. Circle _true_ or _false_ after each sentence.

1. Mother's Day is the second Sunday in May. **(True)** **False**

2. Fathers and grandfathers receive flowers on Father's Day. **True** **False**

3. Americans show their love for their fathers in June. **True** **False**

4. Mothers often have breakfast in bed on Mother's Day. **True** **False**

5. Children give cards and gifts to their fathers on Father's Day. **True** **False**

6. Fathers usually work on Father's Day. **True** **False**

7. Many mothers receive gifts on Mother's Day. **True** **False**

8. Florists sell a lot of flowers on the days before Father's Day. **True** **False**

Now show your answers to another student. Are your answers the same or different? Why?

B. One word in each sentence is wrong. Find the word and cross it out. Then write the correct word.

1. The second Sunday in May is ~~Father's~~ *Mother's* Day.

2. People who see far away call their mothers on the telephone to wish them a "Happy Mother's Day."

3. Mother does not rest on Mother's Day.

4. Many families serve mothers dinner on a tray in bed on Mother's Day.

5. Mothers and grandfathers receive gifts on Father's Day.

6. Father's Day is the second Sunday in June.

7. Mothers do a lot of business on the days before Mother's Day.

8. Many families have brunch in a kitchen on Mother's Day.

2 New Words

Choose one of the following words to complete each sentence. You can work with a classmate.

brunch   florists   tray   business
corsage   relaxation   express

1. People ___express___ their love for their parents on Mother's Day and Father's Day.

2. Telephone companies do a lot of _____ on Mother's Day.

3. Father's Day is a day of _____ for fathers and grandfathers.

4. Many families have _____ in a restaurant on Father's Day.

5. A few days before Mother's Day, many people buy plants from _____.

6. When mothers have breakfast in bed, they usually eat from a _____.

7. Grandmothers often wear a _____ on Mother's Day.

3 More Word Work

A. Find these words in the story about Mother's Day and Father's Day. Draw a line under them. Then look for the synonyms of these words in the story. Circle the synonyms. Write the synonyms here.

1. express ___show___   4. rest _____

2. gifts _____   5. also _____

3. pretty _____

B. Find the words. Some words go across. Some words go down.

```
T R P R E S E N T H E R M
F L O R I S T R A P R E S
O B M F L O R M O T H E R
B R A L O V A G R A N D E
R U Y R E L Y J U N E A P
E N C B R U G U O I T H F
A C O T H G I N O I T B L
K G R A N D F A T H E R O
F I S T E A K C H P F U W
A F A L O V E H E R L N E
S T G D F A T L R E O C R
T R E L A X A T I O N H S
```

Breakfast
Brunch
Corsage
Florist
Flowers
Gift
Grandfather
June
Love
May
Mother
Present
Relaxation
Tray

4 Content Review

With a classmate, complete the sentences. Fill each blank with one word.

Parents are very important people. Americans show their _love_ for their parents on Mother's _____ and Father's Day. Mother's Day is the second _____ in May. This is the day people _____ cards, flowers, and gifts to their _____ and grandmothers. Many families have brunch or _____ in a restaurant to celebrate Mother's Day.

Father's Day is the third Sunday in _____. This is a day of relaxation for _____ and grandfathers. They receive presents and have their _____ foods for dinner.

5 Discussion

What are the answers to these questions? Discuss your answers with another student.

1. What is the date of Mother's Day this year?
2. How do families usually celebrate Mother's Day?
3. Why do florists do a lot of business during the days before Mother's Day?
4. Where do many mothers have breakfast on Mother's Day?
5. When do people express their love for their grandfathers?
6. How do people who live far away show their love for their mothers on Mother's Day?
7. When is Father's Day?
8. What do people do to celebrate Father's Day?
9. Why are mothers and fathers important?
10. Does your country have special days to honor mothers and fathers? When?

6 Writing

A. Make a list of things parents do to help their children.

_____

_____

_____

_____

_____

B. Complete this sentence and write a little story about your mother or father.

The best day I spent with my mother (or father) was

_____

_____

_____

_____

7 Think and Discuss

Think about this question. Then discuss your ideas with the class.

A famous American writer, James Russell Lowell, once said, "The best academy, a mother's knee." What do you think this means?

RONALD K
HALL

LT COL

US AIR FORCE

VIETNAM

MEMORIAL DAY

Look at the month of May on a calendar. What is the date of Memorial Day?

Where are these people?

What are they doing?

Learn these words with your teacher.

weekend   military   grave
sunshine   dead

Memorial Day

In most states, the last Monday in May is Memorial Day. This is not a very happy day. Memorial Day is a national holiday for Americans to remember and honor their dead friends and relatives, especially soldiers and sailors who died in wars.

On Memorial Day, many people visit cemeteries and put flowers on the graves of their friends and relatives. People decorate the graves of soldiers and sailors with small American flags, too. Many cities have parades, patriotic programs, and ceremonies on Memorial Day. Near Washington, D.C., the president honors dead soldiers and sailors in a military ceremony at Arlington National Cemetery.

Many people like Memorial Day because there is a three-day weekend—Saturday, Sunday, and Memorial Day. Memorial Day is the beginning of the summer vacation season. On this day, most public parks and beaches open for the summer. People like to have warm weather and sunshine on Memorial Day. They like to have picnics or go to the beach on this holiday.

1 Comprehension

A. Circle _true_ or _false_ after each sentence.

1. Memorial Day is in May.   (True)   False
2. Memorial Day is a happy holiday.   True   False
3. Americans visit soldiers and sailors on Memorial Day.   True   False
4. People put flowers on graves on Memorial Day.   True   False
5. Many cities have parades on the last Monday in May.   True   False
6. Americans give flags to soldiers on Memorial Day.   True   False
7. People do not like to have good weather on Memorial Day.   True   False

Now show your answers to another student. Are your answers the same or different? Why?

B. One word in each sentence is wrong. Find the word and cross it out. Then write the correct word.

1. The last Monday in ~~June~~ *May* is Memorial Day.
2. Memorial Day is a holiday for Americans to forget their dead friends and relatives.
3. Many people visit beaches and put flowers on the graves of their friends and relatives.
4. People decorate the graves of soldiers with large American flags.
5. Many people like Memorial Day because they have a four-day weekend.
6. Most public parks and beaches open for the winter vacation season on Memorial Day.

2 New Words

Choose one of the following words to complete each sentence. You can work with a classmate.

military   sunshine   dead
weekend   graves

1. Many families spend the ___*weekend*___ at the beach.

2. People put flags on the _____ of American soldiers and sailors.

3. Americans remember their _____ friends and relatives on Memorial Day.

4. There is always a ceremony in _____ cemeteries on Memorial Day.

5. People usually like to have good weather and _____ at the beach.

3 More Word Work

A. Look at these words. Look for the opposites of these words in the story "Memorial Day." Circle the opposites. Then write the opposites here.

1. big _____*small*_____   4. first _____
2. cool _____   5. forget _____
3. end _____   6. sad _____

B. Cross out the word that does not belong.

1. sailor   ~~season~~   soldier   war
2. picnic   dead   cemetery   grave
3. park   beach   president   cemetery
4. friend   flag   relative   sailor
5. summer   sunshine   soldier   flower

4 Content Review

With a classmate, complete the sentences. Fill each blank with one word.

Memorial Day is the last Monday in ____*May*____. On this national holiday, people go to _____ to decorate the graves of relatives with _____. People put small American flags on the _____ of soldiers also.

Memorial Day is the _____ of the summer vacation season. If the _____ is warm, people have picnics or _____ to the beach.

5 Discussion

What are the answers to these questions? Discuss your answers with another student.

1. When is Memorial Day?
2. What is the date of Memorial Day this year?
3. Who do Americans remember on Memorial Day?
4. Why do many people buy flowers on Memorial Day?
5. When do people in your country remember and honor dead relatives?
6. Is there a special day to honor dead soldiers in your country? When is it?
7. What are you going to do on Memorial Day this year?
8. Do you like three-day weekends? Why or why not?

6 Writing

A. Write five things that Americans do on Memorial Day.

Example: *Many people go to patriotic programs.*

1. _____

2. _____

3. _____

4. _____

5. _____

Now write what you are going to do on Memorial Day.

_____

_____

_____

_____

B. Put the words in the right order.

1. *The last Monday in May is Memorial Day.* _____

   Day   in   the   Monday   Memorial   is   last   May

2. _____

   holiday   very   it   not   happy   a   is

3. _____

   relatives   their   of   decorate   the   graves   people

4. _____

   flags   of   soldiers   put   the   on   people   graves

5. _____

   cities   many   are   in   parades   there

6. _____

   beaches   go   people   and   parks   to

C. People remember their dead friends and relatives on Memorial Day. Read this story.

My Classmate Martha

I remember my high school classmate Martha very well. She was very smart and pretty. We studied in class together. After school was over, we played Ping-Pong, went swimming, and did our homework together. One day she was in a car accident and died. I was very surprised and sad. I'll never forget my classmate Martha. She was my best friend.

Now write a story about someone you remember.

_____

_____

_____

_____

_____

_____

_____

7 Think and Discuss

Think about these questions. Then discuss your ideas with the class.

A. Do you think that it is important for people to remember their dead relatives? Why or why not?

B. On what other holiday do Americans remember dead soldiers and sailors?

INDEPENDENCE DAY

Look at the month of July on a calendar. What is the date of Independence Day?

What are the colors of the American flag?

Learn these words with your teacher.

business	independent	cookout
tax	free	

Independence Day

Independence day in the United States is July 4th. This is one of the most important national holidays of the year. It is the birthday of the United States.

The independence of the United States began in 1776. Until that time, the United States belonged to England. In 1776, many Americans were unhappy. They did not like to pay high taxes to England. They did not like English laws. Americans wanted their country to be free and independent. They declared independence from England on July 4, 1776.

Independence Day is a patriotic holiday. Many families and businesses put up American flags to celebrate this day. Decorations at public ceremonies are red, white, and blue—the colors of the flag. This holiday has two names: Independence Day and the Fourth of July.

Independence Day is a summer holiday. Almost everyone has the day off from work. Many families and friends spend the day at the beach or the park. Others have picnics and cookouts. Most cities and towns have parades, patriotic programs, concerts, and, at night, beautiful fireworks.

1 Comprehension

A. Circle <u>true</u> or <u>false</u> after each sentence.

1. July 4th is Independence Day in the
   United States.   (True)   False
2. England belonged to the United States
   until 1776.   True   False
3. The Fourth of July is a patriotic holiday.   True   False
4. Independence Day is in the spring.   True   False
5. Americans celebrate Independence Day
   with flags, parades, and fireworks.   True   False
6. Almost everybody works on the Fourth
   of July.   True   False
7. Independence Day decorations are red,
   white, and green.   True   False ✓

**Now show your answers to another student. Are your
answers the same or different? Why?**

**B. One word in each sentence is wrong. Find the word
and cross it out. Then write the correct word.**

1. Independence Day in the United States is ~~June~~ *July* 4th.
2. The United States belonged to France until 1776.
3. Americans did not like to pay fireworks to England.
4. Many families pay up American flags to celebrate
   Independence Day.
5. Decorations are usually red, yellow, and blue.
6. Independence Day is a summer vacation.
7. Many families declare the day at the beach.

2 New Words

Choose one of the following words to complete each sentence. You can work with a classmate.

free   independent   taxes
cookouts   businesses

1. Many _businesses_ do not open on Independence Day.

2. Before 1776, Americans had to pay _____ to England.

3. The United States was not a _____ and independent country before 1776.

4. Americans wanted their country to be _____.

5. Many people have _____ or go to the beach on July 4th.

3 More Word Work

A. Circle the words that you feel go with the celebration of Independence Day.

(beach)	ceremony	June	red
fish	parade	concert	flag
blue	train	picnic	fireworks
snow	restaurant	white	cookout
radio	green	spring	milk

B. Complete the puzzle.

Across

1. The ____ of the United States is red, white, and blue.
3. Most cities end Fourth of July ceremonies with ____.
4. Independence Day is the most important ____ holiday of the year.
5. The Fourth of July is ____ Day in the United States.
7. Americans did not want to ____ taxes to England.
9. The United States ____ to England until 1776.

Down

1. Americans wanted to live in a ____ and independent country.
2. July 4th is the ____ of the United States.
6. Americans declared their independence from ____ on July 4, 1776.
7. Many businesses ____ up American flags to celebrate Independence Day.
8. Independence Day decorations are usually ____, white, and blue.

4 Content Review

With a classmate, complete the sentences. Fill each blank with one word.

In the United States, the ____Fourth____ of July is a very patriotic holiday. It is _____ Day. It is the birthday of the _____ States. Many people put up _____ to celebrate this holiday. Many families and friends _____ the day at the beach. Cities celebrate with _____, patriotic ceremonies, and concerts. Celebrations usually end with _____ at night.

5 Discussion

What are the answers to these questions? Discuss your answers with another student.

1. When is Independence Day in the United States?
2. How do Americans celebrate Independence Day?
3. How old is the United States?
4. What are the colors of the flag of the United States?
5. Does your country have a celebration like Independence Day? When is it?
6. How do people in your country celebrate this day?
7. How are you going to celebrate Independence Day this year?

6 Writing

Write five things that Americans do on the Fourth of July.

Example: *Many people have picnics.*

_____

_____

_____

_____

_____

Now write how people celebrate a similar holiday in your country.

_____

_____

_____

_____

_____

7 Think and Discuss

Think about this question. Then discuss your ideas with the class.

Independence Day is a patriotic holiday. What other patriotic holidays do Americans celebrate?

Answer Key

Holidays
Pages 6–13

Comprehension
A. 1. yes 2. yes 3. no 4. yes 5. no
6. no 7. no
B. 1. ~~schools~~/people 2. ~~picnics~~/offices
3. ~~week~~/month 4. ~~religious~~/national
5. ~~friends~~/immigrants 6. ~~sad~~/happy

New Words
1. religious 2. events 3. celebrations
4. celebrate 5. immigrants 6. picnic

More Word Work
A.

B. 1. American 2. event 3. picnic
4. parties 5. work

Content Review
Everybody likes holidays. Most
holidays are <u>special</u> days to remember
important <u>people</u> and events. On national
holidays <u>banks</u>, offices, and schools do not
<u>open</u>. Labor Day is a national <u>holiday</u>.
Christmas and Easter are important
<u>religious</u> holidays. A holiday is a
time for <u>celebration</u>.

Labor Day
Pages 14–21

Comprehension
A. 1. yes 2. yes 3. no 4. yes 5. yes
6. no 7. no 8. yes
B. 1. ~~Wednesday~~/Monday
2. ~~schools~~/workers 3. ~~remember~~/work
4. ~~stores~~/offices 5. ~~work~~/picnics
6. ~~parades~~/sales

New Words
1. rest 2. fun 3. honors 4. return
5. sales 6. Labor unions

More Word Work
A. 1. rest 2. cold 3. close 4. last
B. 1. engineer 2. weather 3. work
4. labor 5. last 6. secretary

Content Review
Labor Day is the first <u>Monday</u> in
September. It is the <u>holiday</u> that honors
workers every year. Many <u>people</u> do not
work on Labor <u>Day</u>. Schools and banks do
not <u>open</u>. Many people have fun at <u>picnics</u>
and barbecues. Students often return to
<u>school</u> the day after Labor Day.

Columbus Day
Pages 22–29

Comprehension
A. 1. yes 2. no 3. yes 4. yes 5. no
6. yes 7. no 8. yes
B. 1. ~~India~~/America 2. ~~ships~~/spices
3. ~~long~~/short 4. ~~Italy~~/Spain
5. ~~America~~/Europe 6. ~~two~~/three
7. ~~August~~/October 8. ~~Indians~~/people

New Words
1. explorers 2. island 3. travel
4. dangerous 5. sailor 6. spices

More Word Work
A.

B. 1. Asia 2. island 3. spice 4. king
5. trip 6. land

Content Review
Columbus Day honors Christopher
Columbus's first <u>trip</u> to America. Columbus
was born in <u>Italy</u>. Before his trip, he was a
<u>sailor</u>. Columbus wanted to find a short
<u>way</u> to India by sea. He left <u>Spain</u> with
three ships. He arrived at an <u>island</u> on
October 12, 1492. Columbus called the
people there <u>Indians</u> because he thought

that he was in <u>India</u>. After Columbus's trip,
many Europeans came to <u>live</u> in America.

Writing
B. 1. Italian 2. Spanish 3. English
4. French 5. Indian 6. Chinese
7. Mexican 8. Vietnamese 9. Brazilian
10. Korean
C. 1. When is Columbus Day?
2. Where was Columbus born?
3. What did Europeans like to buy
from India?
4. What did the king and queen of Spain
give Columbus for his trip?
5. When did Columbus arrive at an island
near North America?

Halloween
Pages 30–37

Comprehension
A. 1. yes 2. yes 3. no 4. no 5. yes
6. yes
B. 1. ~~August~~/October 2. ~~eat~~/wear
3. ~~candles~~/ghosts 4. ~~symbols~~/costumes
5. ~~blue~~/black 6. ~~fruit~~/bags
7. ~~costume~~/jack-o'-lantern
8. ~~bag~~/pumpkin

New Words
1. costumes 2. decorations 3. candle
4. pumpkin 5. Adults 6. symbol

More Word Work
A. 1. adults 2. face 3. bag 4. black
5. symbol
B. Across
3. October 9. decorations 11. bags
14. pumpkin 15. Halloween
Down
1. fruit 2. face 4. candle 5. masks
6. carry 7. party 8. boys
10. costume 12. wear 13. door

Content Review
Americans celebrate Halloween on
October 31 <u>every</u> year. Boys and girls
wear masks and <u>costumes</u> on this special
day. At night, children <u>knock</u> on their
neighbors' doors and shout, "Trick or treat!"
Then the neighbors put <u>candy</u> or fruit in the
children's bags.
The <u>jack-o'-lantern</u> is a popular symbol
of Halloween. <u>Orange</u> and black are the
traditional colors for Halloween.

Veterans Day
Pages 38–45

Comprehension
A. 1. yes 2. yes 3. no 4. yes 5. yes
   6. no
B. 1. ~~December~~/November 2. ~~stores~~/wars
   3. ~~uniforms~~/flags 4. ~~religious~~/national
   5. ~~black~~/blue 6. ~~cemeteries~~/parades
   7. ~~uniforms~~/sales 8. ~~work~~/rest

New Words
1. Soldiers 2. veterans 3. peace
4. patriotic 5. parades 6. uniforms
7. war

More Word Work

B. 1. peace 2. out 3. November
   4. sales 5. wear 6. stay

Content Review
Veterans Day is a national holiday. Veterans are people who fought in wars. The special colors for Veterans Day are red, white, and blue. Americans honor veterans and celebrate peace on this day. Many veterans march in parades. Many people put American flags in front of their homes. Veterans Day is an important, patriotic holiday.

Writing
1. Veterans Day is in November.
2. Veterans Day is a patriotic holiday.
3. Many veterans march in parades.
4. People put flags in front of their homes.
5. Veterans are people who fought in wars.

Thanksgiving Day
Pages 46–53

Comprehension
A. 1. yes 2. yes 3. no 4. yes 5. no
B. 1. ~~first~~/fourth 2. ~~months~~/years
   3. ~~America~~/England 4. ~~spring~~/winter
   5. ~~immigrants~~/Americans 6. ~~hunt~~/celebrate 7. ~~friends~~/families

New Words
1. showed 2. immigrants
3. died 4. turkey 5. Native Americans

More Word Work
A. 1. Pilgrim 2. dinner 3. hunt
   4. Thanksgiving
B. Across
   3. Massachusetts 6. turkey 7. years
   9. good 12. immigrants
   Down
   1. hunt 2. Thanksgiving 4. sauce
   5. Thursday 8. November 10. corn
   11. fish
C. Places: England, America, Massachusetts, church
   Foods: turkey, corn, fish, cranberry sauce, sweet potato, pumpkin pie

Content Review
Americans give thanks for the good things in their lives on Thanksgiving Day. This popular holiday is always the fourth Thursday in November. The Pilgrims celebrated the first Thanksgiving Day with Native Americans over 300 years ago. Most Americans today celebrate this holiday with their families. The traditional foods for Thanksgiving dinner are: turkey, cranberry sauce, sweet potatoes, corn, and pumpkin pie.

Writing
B. 1. When did the Pilgrims come from England?
   2. When do Americans celebrate Thanksgiving Day?
   3. Where did the Pilgrims celebrate the first Thanksgiving Day?
   4. Who did the Native Americans show how to hunt? (or) Who showed the Pilgrims how to hunt?

Hanukkah
Pages 54–61

Comprehension
A. 1. yes 2. yes 3. no 4. no
   5. yes 6. no 7. no
B. 1. ~~six~~/eight 2. ~~Songs~~/Lights
   3. ~~morning~~/night 4. ~~Parents~~/Children
   5. ~~summer~~/winter 6. ~~games~~/foods

New Words
1. Jewish 2. get together 3. hymn
4. pancakes 5. applesauce 6. No wonder

More Word Work
A.
```
D L I G H T S G C A P H
E H A N U K K A H P A N
C Y P O T A T M E P N U
E M P A N C A E E L C A
M O L C H E E S S E A K
B G E H Y M N K E S K K
E K S O X L I G H A E A
M C A N D L E S K C I L
O C U M O N E G I F T S
N D C A K P O T A T O Y
E I E W I S H C A N D L
Y A V D E C E M B E R Z
```
B. 1. festival 2. night 3. everybody
   4. enjoy 5. small 6. gifts 7. also

Content Review
Eight nights every winter, Jewish people celebrate Hanukkah. Families get together each night and light candles. Then they usually eat potato pancakes and applesauce. Children like this festival very much. They play traditional games. Their parents give them money and small gifts. Another name for Hanukkah is the Festival of Lights.

Writing
A. 1. Children have fun playing games.
   2. Parents give money to children.
   3. Families light candles and sing songs.
   4. Jewish families celebrate Hanukkah for eight nights.
   5. Another name for Hanukkah is the Festival of Lights. (or) The Festival of Lights is another name for Hanukkah.

Christmas
Pages 62–69

Comprehension
A. 1. yes 2. no 3. yes 4. yes 5. yes
   6. yes 7. no
B. 1. ~~sad~~/happy 2. ~~years~~/weeks
   3. ~~trees~~/cards 4. ~~white~~/red 5. ~~wish~~/sing
   6. ~~school~~/church

New Words
1. ornaments 2. Christmas carols
3. decorate 4. plants 5. wrap
6. Christmas cards

More Word Work

A.

B. green, church, gifts, shopping, tree, turkey, ornaments, family, red, cards, music, fruitcake

Content Review

Christmas is a very happy time of the year. Families decorate trees with lights and ornaments. People sing traditional songs called Christmas carols. People wrap gifts in pretty paper and give them to their friends and relatives. They wish each other "Merry Christmas." Many families go to church and then, at home, open their gifts and have a traditional Christmas dinner.

Writing

A. 1. What are the traditional colors for Christmas?
2. What are Christmas carols?
3. Where do people put Christmas gifts?
4. When do preparations for Christmas begin?
5. Where do many families go on Christmas morning?
6. When do people send Christmas cards?

Kwanzaa
Pages 70–77

Comprehension

A. 1. yes 2. yes 3. no 4. yes
5. no 6. no 7. yes

B. 1. ~~November~~/December 2. ~~after~~/before
3. ~~blue~~/black 4. tables/~~candles~~
5. ~~morning~~/evening 6. ~~think~~/wear
7. ~~set~~/sing

New Words

1. community 2. culture 3. proud 4. set
5. principle 6. future

More Word Work

A. 1. in 2. to 3. of 4. of 5. in 6. about

B. fruit, music, gift, red, candle, December, song, black, party, vegetables, culture, family, seven

Content Review

Every year, from December 26 to January 1, African-American children light candles at Kwanzaa festivals. Kwanzaa is a celebration of the history and culture of black people in the United States. At Kwanzaa time, many people wear African clothes and children receive gifts. People talk about important principles of the African-American community. They also underline{sing} songs and dance.

Writing

A. 1. When is Kwanzaa?
2. Where do people celebrate Kwanzaa?
3. When does the family decorate the house?
4. What do children receive at Kwanzaa celebrations?
5. When does everyone sing and dance?

New Year's Celebrations
Pages 78–87

Comprehension

A. 1. yes 2. yes 3. no 4. yes 5. no
6. yes 7. yes 8. no

B. 1. ~~Day~~/Eve 2. ~~horns~~/hats
3. ~~parades~~/seconds 4. ~~confetti~~/horns
5. ~~work~~/rest 6. ~~hug~~/eat
7. ~~whistles~~/promises 8. ~~start~~/stop

New Words

1. confetti 2. whistles 3. resolutions
4. habits 5. luck 6. hug

More Word Work

Across
3. football 6. restaurant 9. make 11. hug
12. eat 13. wish 14. count 16. habits
Down
1. good 2. year 4. time 5. day
6. resolutions 7. rest 8. throw
10. whistles 12. eve 15. wear 17. TV

Content Review

The beginning of the new year is a happy time in the United States. December 31 is not a holiday, but at night there are many parties in homes and restaurants. At midnight, people make noise with horns and whistles. They kiss, hug, and wish each other "Happy New Year."

In New York City, people celebrate in the streets. At 11:59, they count the seconds until midnight. Then everybody welcomes the underline{new} year with lots of noise.

Writing

B. 1. People go to parties at night.
2. Almost nobody works on New Year's Day.

3. I will stop smoking this year.
4. People want to stop bad habits.
5. New Year's Eve parties are lots of fun.

Chinese New Year
Pages 88–95

Comprehension

A. 1. no 2. yes 3. no 4. no
5. yes 6. yes 7. yes

B. 1. ~~schools~~/homes 2. ~~costumes~~/fruit
3. ~~after~~/before 4. ~~boxes~~/envelopes
5. ~~end~~/beginning 6. ~~eat~~/dragon

New Words

1. bills 2. envelopes 3. explode 4. lion
5. dragon 6. firecrackers

More Word Work

A. gifts, orange, parade, firecrackers, food, flowers, dragon, bills, lion, fruit

B. Across
3. firecracker 8. parade 9. lion
11. dragon 12. Chinese
Down
1. money 2. luck 4. red 5. clean
6. explode 7. year 10. oranges

Content Review

The most important festival of the Chinese people is the celebration of Chinese New Year. There are celebrations in many cities in the United States. People wear new clothes to celebrate the new year. underline{Children} receive gifts of money in small, underline{red} envelopes. Families celebrate with a special underline{dinner}. The popular event is always the underline{parade} with noisy firecrackers and a large underline{dragon}.

Martin Luther King, Jr., Day
Pages 96–103

Comprehension

A. 1. true 2. true 3. false 4. false
5. true 6. true

B. 1. ~~rich~~/poor 2. ~~theater~~/church
3. ~~protests~~/rights 4. ~~separated~~/wrote
5. ~~wrote~~/received 6. ~~stopped~~/started
7. ~~October~~/January

New Words

1. equal rights 2. restrooms 3. minister
4. leader 5. laws 6. speeches

More Word Work

A. Across
2. protests 8. peace 9. change
12. Congress 13. laws 14. minister
15. hotels
Down
1. black 3. rights 4. eat 5. schools
6. speeches 7. January 10. prize

11. white

B. 1. poor **2.** angry **3.** many
    4. young, new **5.** same **6.** peaceful
    7. started **8.** received

Content Review

Martin Luther King, Jr., was a <u>minister</u> of a church in Alabama. When he was young, <u>laws</u> separated black people from white <u>people</u> in the United States. Martin Luther King did not like these laws. He wanted everyone to have equal <u>rights</u>. He wanted all people to live together in <u>peace</u>. Martin Luther King led people in peaceful <u>protests</u> and made many speeches. He received the Nobel Peace <u>Prize</u> in 1964. The third Monday in <u>January</u> is a national holiday honoring this important American leader.

Writing

A. 1. Congress changed many laws.
    2. Black people did not have equal rights.
    3. The third Monday in January is a national holiday.
    4. Martin Luther King wrote books and made speeches.
    5. He wanted all people to live together in peace.
    6. Many people were very happy about the new laws.

Carnival and Mardi Gras
Pages 104–111

Comprehension

A. 1. true **2.** true **3.** false **4.** false
    5. true **6.** false **7.** true **8.** true
    9. false

B. 1. ~~England~~/France **2.** ~~week~~/month
    3. ~~sing~~/play **4.** ~~first~~/last
    5. ~~floats~~/costumes **6.** ~~parties~~/parades
    7. ~~month~~/year

New Words

1. elegant **2.** floats **3.** jazz **4.** clowns
5. full **6.** spicy **7.** balls

More Word Work

B. 1. spicy **2.** clown **3.** February
    4. world **5.** Carnival

Content Review

Carnival is a festival of <u>music</u>, parades, and costumes. Americans celebrate <u>Carnival</u> every year in New Orleans, Louisiana. The festival <u>begins</u> in January and continues for a month or more.

The <u>last</u> day of Carnival is Mardi <u>Gras</u>. This is the day people <u>wear</u> masks and costumes in the streets. Everybody <u>has</u> fun watching the parades and dancing until <u>midnight</u>.

Immigrants brought the carnival celebration from <u>France</u> to Louisiana over 200 years ago.

Writing

1. Americans celebrate Carnival in New Orleans.
2. Mardi Gras is a festival in New Orleans.
3. People have fun dancing until midnight.
4. People wear costumes on Mardi Gras.
5. Many visitors come to Louisiana to enjoy Carnival.

Valentine's Day
Pages 112–119

Comprehension

A. 1. false **2.** true **3.** false **4.** false
    5. true **6.** true **7.** true **8.** false

B. 1. ~~sweethearts~~/valentines **2.** ~~flower~~/heart
    3. ~~Funny~~/Romantic **4.** ~~books~~/flowers
    5. ~~sad~~/funny

New Words

1. romantic **2.** couples **3.** chocolate
4. heart **5.** messages **6.** friendship

More Word Work

A. flowers, gift, romantic, card, love, heart, sweetheart, friendship, girlfriend, red, February

B. 1. of **2.** on **3.** of **4.** to, on **5.** to, at

Content Review

On February 14, people send cards called <u>valentines</u> to their friends. Many valentines are <u>romantic</u>. They have messages of love. Other <u>valentines</u> have very funny pictures and messages. <u>Children</u> give funny valentines to their classmates at <u>school</u>. Almost all valentines have a red <u>heart</u>, the traditional symbol of love. Chocolate <u>candy</u> and flowers are popular Valentine's Day gifts.

Presidents' Day
Pages 120–127

Comprehension

A. 1. true **2.** false **3.** true **4.** true
    5. false **6.** false **7.** true

B. 1. ~~three~~/two **2.** ~~March~~/February
    3. ~~Abraham~~/George **4.** ~~capital~~/country
    5. ~~penny~~/quarter **6.** ~~city~~/country
    7. ~~states~~/slaves **8.** ~~quarter~~/penny

New Words

1. president **2.** independence **3.** dollar bill
4. penny **5.** capital **6.** slaves **7.** quarter

More Word Work

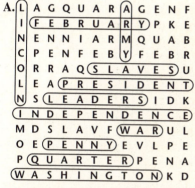

B. George Washington: February, war, president, quarter, famous, capital, leader, independence
    Abraham Lincoln: February, war, slaves, president, famous, penny, leader

Content Review

The third Monday in February is <u>Presidents'</u> Day. This national holiday honors George <u>Washington</u> and Abraham Lincoln. George Washington was the first <u>president</u> of the United States. A picture of George Washington is on the <u>quarter</u>. Abraham Lincoln was the sixteenth president. He <u>freed</u> the slaves. His picture is on the five-dollar <u>bill</u>. Washington and Lincoln were important leaders in <u>American</u> history.

Writing

B. 1. Who was George Washington?
    2. When is his birthday?
    3. Who freed the slaves?
    4. When was he born?
    5. Where can we see a picture of George Washington?
    6. When is Presidents' Day?

Saint Patrick's Day
Pages 128–135

Comprehension
A. 1. true 2. true 3. false 4. false
5. false 6. true 7. true 8. false
B. 1. ~~student~~/priest 2. ~~schools~~/churches
3. ~~May~~/March 4. ~~blue~~/green
5. ~~cabbage~~/shamrock 6. ~~five~~/three
7. ~~wear~~/play 8. ~~shamrocks~~/cabbage

New Words
1. shamrock 2. Irish 3. Ireland 4. hero
5. boiled 6. priest

More Word Work
A.
```
B I R E L P A R A D S
E R A C K V P L E V H
F E S H A M R O C K A
O L G R P R I E S I M
C A R I K B E F Q R G
A N E S M U S I C S R
B D E T O D T J P S E
Y M N I B E E F N H D
S U P A R A D E H T K
H S T N C A B B A G E
G R E I R E L A M U S
```

Content Review
Many years ago, Saint Patrick was a priest in Ireland. Saint Patrick is an important hero of Ireland because he built many churches for the Irish people.
Saint Patrick's Day is March 17. Many people like to wear something green on Saint Patrick's Day. Radio stations play Irish music and many cities have parades to celebrate this day.

Writing
B. 1. Who is an important hero of Ireland?
2. What is the national flower of Ireland?
3. What is a shamrock?
4. Why is Saint Patrick famous?
5. What do radio stations do on Saint Patrick's Day?
6. Where are there big Saint Patrick's Day celebrations?

The Cherry Blossom Festival
Pages 136–143

Comprehension
A. 1. true 2. false 3. true 4. true
5. false 6. true 7. true 8. false
B. 1. ~~birds~~/blossoms 2. ~~fruit~~/flowers
3. ~~summer~~/spring 4. ~~bring~~/take
5. ~~festivals~~/trees 6. ~~parades~~/friendship
7. ~~concert~~/capital

New Words
1. cherry 2. tourists 3. blossoms
4. annual 5. photographs 6. Photography

More Word Work
A. flowers, gift, parade, pink, concert, capital, photography, spring, tree, Japan, tourist, friendship
B. 1. in 2. to 3. of 4. from 5. of 6. of

Content Review
Every spring, thousands of tourists come to Washington, D.C., to enjoy the city's Cherry Blossom Festival. Cherry blossoms are the flowers of cherry trees. Pretty cherry blossoms appear on about 3,000 trees every March or April. Washington's cherry trees are a gift from Japan. These beautiful trees are a symbol of friendship between Japan and the United States. Their blossoms make Washington, D.C., very beautiful every spring.

Easter
Pages 144–151

Comprehension
A. 1. true 2. true 3. true 4. false 5. true
6. false 7. true 8. false 9. false
B. 1. ~~national~~/religious 2. ~~evening~~/morning
3. ~~wash~~/wear 4. ~~birds~~/eggs
5. ~~winter~~/spring 6. ~~children~~/flowers

New Words
1. Bunny 2. baskets 3. happiness
4. nature 5. lily

More Word Work
A. **Across**
1. nature 3. flowers 7. baskets
8. church 10. bunny 11. March
Down
2. religious 4. eggs 5. Sunday
6. wear 8. candy 9. children
B. birds, plants, leaves, eggs
C. spring, March, morning, year
D. Nature: flowers, lilies, animals, bunny, vegetables
Time: April, winter, afternoon, Sunday

Content Review
Easter is a very religious holiday in March or April. On Easter Sunday, many people go to church early in the morning. Easter is the day that children color eggs for their Easter baskets. Adults give candy or flowers to their friends and relatives. Many radios stations play religious music. Everyone likes to wear new clothes on Easter Sunday because it is a very happy holiday.

Cinco de Mayo
Pages 152–159

Comprehension
A. 1. true 2. true 3. false 4. false
5. true 6. true 7. false
B. 1. ~~French~~/Mexican
2. ~~northern~~/southwestern
3. ~~blue~~/green 4. ~~dance~~/play
5. ~~celebrate~~/wear 6. ~~buy~~/sell
7. ~~France~~/Mexico

New Words
1. vendors 2. victory 3. region 4. battle
5. southwestern 6. fireworks

More Word Work
A.
```
M U S I C F V I C T D S
E S O L D I E R S E C O
X C U K O R N S V K A L
B A T T L E D O N B L D
A L H U I W O N C P I I
T I W O N O R G T A F E
T F E Y C R E S O R O V
V O S O U K Y L R A R E
E R T H K S M A Y D F N
Q N E S O U T H W E I D
D I R E G I O N A R M Y
O A N S O M E X I C O K
```

B. 1. vendor 2. food 3. southwestern
4. region 5. victory

Content Review
The Cinco de Mayo festival is very popular in the southwestern region of the United States. This region was once part of Mexico. During the festival, bands in parades play Mexican music. Many children and adults wear Mexican clothes. After the parade, people enjoy other activities in a park. They buy Mexican foods and drinks from vendors. The festivities usually end with a show of fireworks in the evening.

Writing
A. 1. Many Mexican-Americans live in California.
2. Many cities have parades on May fifth.
3. Bands in parades play Mexican music.
4. There are many activities in a large park.
5. People enjoy Mexican songs and dances.
6. The festivities end with a show of fireworks.
B. 1. What does Cinco de Mayo mean?
2. What color is the Mexican flag?
3. Where do many Mexican-Americans live?
4. When did Mexican soldiers win a battle against the French army?

5. What do many children wear on Cinco de Mayo?

Mother's Day and Father's Day
Pages 160–167

Comprehension
A. 1. true 2. false 3. true 4. true 5. true
6. false 7. true 8. false

B. 1. ~~Father's~~/Mother's 2. ~~see~~/live
3. ~~rest~~/work 4. ~~dinner~~/breakfast
5. ~~Mothers~~/Fathers 6. ~~second~~/third
7. ~~Mothers~~/Florists 8. ~~kitchen~~/restaurant

New Words
1. express 2. business 3. relaxation
4. brunch 5. florists 6. tray 7. corsage

More Word Work
A. 1. show 2. presents 3. beautiful
4. relaxation 5. too

B.
```
T R P R E S E N T H E R M
F L O R I S T R A P R E S
O B M F L O R M O T H E R
B R A L O V A G R A N D E
R U Y R E L Y J U N E A P
E N C B R U G U O I T H F
A C O T H G I N O I T B L
K G R A N D F A T H E R O
F I S T E A K C H P F U W
A F A L O V E H E R L N E
S T G D F A T L R E O C R
T R E L A X A T I O N H H
```

Content Review
Parents are very important people. Americans show their <u>love</u> for their parents on Mother's <u>Day</u> and Father's Day. Mother's Day is the second <u>Sunday</u> in May. This is the day people <u>give</u> cards, flowers, and gifts to their <u>mothers</u> and grandmothers. Many families have brunch or <u>dinner</u> in a restaurant to celebrate Mother's Day.

Father's Day is the third Sunday in <u>June</u>. This is a day of relaxation for <u>fathers</u> and grandfathers. They receive presents and have their <u>favorite</u> foods for dinner.

Memorial Day
Pages 168–175

Comprehension
A. 1. true 2. false 3. false 4. true 5. true
6. false 7. false

B. 1. ~~June~~/May 2. ~~forget~~/remember
3. ~~beaches~~/cemeteries 4. ~~large~~/small
5. ~~four-day~~/three-day 6. ~~winter~~/summer

New Words
1. weekend 2. graves 3. dead
4. military 5. sunshine

More Word Work
A. 1. small 2. warm 3. beginning 4. last
5. remember 6. happy

B. 1. season 2. picnic 3. president
4. flag 5. soldier

Content Review
Memorial day is the last Monday in <u>May</u>. On this national holiday, people go to <u>cemeteries</u> to decorate the graves of relatives with <u>flowers</u>. People put small American flags on the <u>graves</u> of soldiers also.

Memorial Day is the <u>beginning</u> of the summer vacation season. If the <u>weather</u> is warm, people have picnics or <u>go</u> to the beach.

Writing
B. 1. The last Monday in May is Memorial Day.
2. It is not a very happy holiday.
3. People decorate the graves of their relatives.
4. People put flags on the graves of soldiers.
5. There are parades in many cities.
6. People go to beaches and parks.

Independence Day
Pages 176–183

Comprehension
A. 1. true 2. false 3. true 4. false
5. true 6. false 7. false

B. 1. ~~June~~/July 2. ~~France~~/England
3. ~~fireworks~~/taxes 4. ~~pay~~/put
5. ~~yellow~~/white 6. ~~vacation~~/holiday
7. ~~declare~~/spend

New Words
1. businesses 2. taxes 3. free
4. independent 5. cookouts

More Word Work
A. beach, ceremony, red, parade, concert, flag, blue, picnic, fireworks, white, cookout

B. **Across**
1. flag 3. fireworks 4. patriotic
5. independence 7. pay 9. belonged
Down
1. free 2. birthday 6. England
7. put 8. red

Content Review
In the United States, the <u>Fourth</u> of July is a very patriotic holiday. It is <u>Independence</u> Day. It is the birthday of the <u>United</u> States. Many people put up <u>flags</u> to celebrate this holiday. Many families and friends <u>spend</u> the day at the beach. Cities celebrate with <u>parades</u>, patriotic ceremonies, and concerts. Celebrations usually end with <u>fireworks</u> at night.